BISON
BOOKS

W9-BMS-710

This Hallowed Ground: Guides to Civil War Battlefields

SERIES EDITORS

Brooks D. Simpson
Arizona State University

Mark Grimsley
The Ohio State University

Steven E. Woodworth
Texas Christian University

CHICKAMAUGA
A BATTLEFIELD GUIDE
BY STEVEN E. WOODWORTH
WITH A SECTION ON
CHATTANOOGA

Cartography by Marcia McLean

•

University of Nebraska Press

Lincoln and London

Library of Congress Cataloging in Publication Data
Woodworth, Steven E.
Chickamauga : a battlefield guide with a section on
Chattanooga / Steven E. Woodworth.
p.   cm. – (This hallowed ground)
Includes bibliographical references (p.   ).
ISBN 0-8032-9802-1 (pbk.: alkaline paper)
1. Chickamauga (Ga.), Battle of, 1863.
2. Chattanooga (Tenn.), Battle of, 1863.
3. Chickamauga and Chattanooga National Military
Park (Ga. and Tenn.) – Guidebooks.   I. Title.   II. Series.
E475.81.W878 1999 973.7′35 – dc21 98-29899 CIP

Contents

Acknowledgments

I take pleasure in acknowledging the help of many who have graciously assisted me in the process of learning, organizing, and writing that produced this guide. My fellow series editors, Mark Grimsley of Ohio State University and Brooks D. Simpson of Arizona State University, have been of great assistance. Mark in particular invested three multi-day study sessions on the battlefield – once with me and twice with a draft of this guide, which he gave a very thorough going over. The final product is much superior thanks to his sharp mind and "infinite capacity for taking pains." Chickamauga and Chattanooga National Military Park chief historian James Ogden gave me a tour of the battlefield, answered many questions, and has been uniformly helpful. Ralph and Erma Woodworth gave the guide manuscript a layman's test drive and provided useful feedback. On various occasions Michael McGinn and the students of my Civil War course at Toccoa Falls College accompanied me on visits to the battlefield and asked thoughtful questions that have helped me sharpen my ability to communicate the story of the battle. To all of them, I extend my warmest thanks. Many of the illustrations reproduced in this book first appeared in *Battles and Leaders of the Civil War*, Robert Underwood Johnson and Clarence Clough Buel, 4 vols. (New York: Century Co., 1887–88). They are identified in the captions by the initials BLCW, followed by their volume and page numbers.

Right: *Reveille.* BLCW 4:475

Introduction

In September 1863 the Union Army of the Cumberland met the Confederate Army of Tennessee in the woods and hardscrabble cornfields of northwest Georgia in one of the most dramatic battles of the Civil War. Chickamauga displayed the valor and toughness of the Civil War soldier—and the alternate brilliance and blundering of his commanders—as well as any conflict in the war. Only at Gettysburg, where considerably more men were present, did a Civil War battle produce a longer casualty list than that of Chickamauga, and Chickamauga was both the largest battle and the only major Confederate victory west of the Appalachians. Chickamauga witnessed the increasing tendency of Civil War soldiers to build fieldworks, a sound instinct for self-preservation that was to become very pronounced in the year and a half of war that remained. It was the last great Confederate offensive that had any remote chance of reversing, at least temporarily, the tide of the war, and it was the last of the great old-fashioned set-piece battles—outside siege lines and prepared positions—before Ulysses S. Grant and William T. Sherman took over the major Union armies and began the relentless drive toward victory that knew neither pause nor retreat—Grant's tenacious "bulldog grip" on Robert E. Lee's Army of Northern Virginia and Sherman's "big Indian war" through Georgia—during 1864. It is a fascinating study.

"Carry me back to Ole Virginny." BLCW 3:420

How to Use This Guide

It is to see that ground that people come to the battle sites; this guide represents an effort to help them understand what they see. It seeks to fill a niche between the overviews of the battle available in pamphlets and handouts and the rather detailed treatment of battle terrain and action offered in several guides, exemplified by the series of U.S. Army War College guides. It is designed for people who are willing to invest a day in examining the battlefield with some care in order to understand how the battle unfolded and why it turned out as it did. Descriptions and maps outline the appearance of the terrain in 1863, the position of the contending forces, and the action in various areas on the field. Although the guide is not an exhaustive treatment of the entire engagement, it explores the major (and some of the not-so-major) engagements that made up the battles of Chickamauga and Chattanooga. Finally, although users of the guide might benefit from examining it prior to a visit to the battlefield, such preparation is not essential: one can pick up the guide, drive out to the battlefield, and begin a tour immediately.

This book has two main sections. The first is a guide to the battlefield of Chickamauga, the second to that of Chattanooga. The Chickamauga guide is divided into 20 stops, each of which will require about 15 to 20 minutes. Thus the main tour of the Chickamauga battlefield should take about six hours. As much as possible, each stop has been designed so as to require you to walk no more than 100 yards from your car. In the guidebook, each stop consists of a section of text "married" to a map. This enables you to visualize the troop dispositions and movements at each stop without having to flip around the guide looking for maps.

The stops follow a standard format: **Directions, Orientation, What Happened, Analysis,** and/or **Vignette.**

The **Directions** tell you how to get from one stop to the next. They not only give you driving instructions but also ask you, once you have reached a given stop, to walk to a precise spot on the battlefield. When driving, keep an eye on your odometer; many distances are given to the nearest tenth of a mile. Occasionally the directions suggest points of interest en route from one stop to another. These always come after the actual driving instructions and are introduced by the italicized words *En route.*

Once you've reached a stop, the **Orientation** section describes the terrain around you so that you can quickly pick out the key landmarks and get your bearings.

What Happened is the heart of each stop. It explains the action succinctly but without becoming simplistic, and whenever possible it explains how the terrain affected the fighting.

Most stops have a section called **Analysis**, which explains why a particular decision was made, why a given attack met with success or failure, and so on. The purpose is to give you additional insight into the battle.

Many stops have a section called **Vignette**, designed to give you an additional emotional understanding of the battle by offering a short eyewitness account or by telling a particularly vivid anecdote.

If you have more than the six hours required to complete the main tour, this guide allows you a variety of options for enriching your battlefield exploration.

Further Exploration sections suggest additional areas to visit and view. Most of these you will reach on foot–including some walks longer than 100 yards–and some will require additional driving. Usually little further explanation will be required for you to appreciate each of these sites beyond what is already given in the stop to which it is attached.

Optional Excursions are in fact additional stops, roughly comparable to the main stops in time required and amount of information provided. Instructions for reaching them are inserted at the appropriate places in the tour, and you will be instructed on where to turn in this guidebook to find the corresponding text and maps. At the end of each optional excursion, directions will route you back onto the main tour.

This guidebook also includes a section offering a brief guide to the few preserved sites of the nearby (and closely related) battle of Chattanooga. The Chattanooga section consists of seven stops. The time required to complete it will vary widely depending on traffic conditions, personal tastes, and driving styles, but you will probably need at least three to four hours.

A few conventions are used in the guidebook to help keep confusion to a minimum. Names and unit designations are used as sparingly as possible while still conveying a solid understanding of the battle. Names of Confederate leaders are in italics. Union corps numbers are given in roman numerals (e.g., XIV Corps). Union divisions and brigades and all Confederate units above the level of regiment are identified by the names of their commanders (e.g. *Cleburne's* division). The full name and rank of each individual is usually given only the first time he is mentioned.

Directions are particularly important in a guidebook, but they can often be confusing. Every effort has been made to render these as clear as possible. At each stop you are asked to face toward a specific, easily identifiable landmark, often a battlefield monument. From that point you may be asked to look to your left or right. To make this as precise as possible, we may sometimes ask you to look to your left front, left, left rear, and so on, according to the system shown below:

straight ahead

left front	*right front*
left	*right*
left rear	*right rear*

behind/directly to the rear

Often, after the relative directions (left, right, etc.), you'll find the ordinal directions (north, south, etc.) in parentheses. The maps can also help you get your bearings.

Although this guidebook is intended primarily for use on the battlefield, it also contains information helpful for further study of the battle. An introductory section at the beginning of the book, "The Road to Chickamauga," places the campaign in the perspective of the war as a whole and describes the action that preceded the battle; a similar section at the beginning of the Chattanooga section fills you in on the action during the two months between the battles; and a section at the end tells what happened after the battle ended. The stops for each day of the battle of Chickamauga are preceded by overviews that outline the day's main developments. Appendixes at the end of the book give the organization of each army (Orders of Battle) and provide general information about Civil War–era armies. Detailed suggestions for further reading are in the back, along with a section on sources that provides attribution for information, interpretations, and quotations used.

We hope you enjoy your battlefield tour of Chickamauga and Chattanooga.

Mark Grimsley,
Brooks D. Simpson, &
Steven E. Woodworth
SERIES EDITORS

Beating the Long Roll. BLCW 4:179

September 19, 1863: Longstreet's troops detrain at Ringgold, Georgia, on their way to join Bragg at Chickamauga Creek. From J. M. Brown, *The Mountain Campaigns in Georgia*, Matthews, Northrup & Co. (Buffalo NY: 1890)

The Road to Chickamauga

By the middle of the third year of the Civil War, the Confederacy's military situation was becoming increasingly critical. The North was eager to press the advantage it held and end the war soon. The South was anxious to reverse its series of disastrous defeats and regain its military equilibrium – and a good deal of lost territory. The result, in part, was the battle of Chickamauga.

Initial Northern strategy in the war had envisioned an ever tighter naval blockade of Southern ports, a Union drive to secure the entire course of the Mississippi River, and several deep penetrations into the heart of the slave states. Two of the most important of these interior targets were the Confederate capital at Richmond and the Southern Unionist enclave of East Tennessee. President Abraham Lincoln, who had high hopes that Southerners loyal to the Union would help restore the entire South to its allegiance, desired intensely to reach and help the East Tennesseeans.

The first two years of the war proved the difficulty of implementing the Northern strategy. Impressive successes by Ulysses S. Grant in the Mississippi Valley came to a halt before the seemingly impregnable fortress town of Vicksburg. The blockade was porous. Repeated "On to Richmond" drives came to grief at the hands of the remarkable Robert E. *Lee*, and in the country's midsection, Lincoln found he could get none of his generals to advance directly toward his cherished goal of liberating East Tennessee. All objected – probably correctly – that rough terrain and lack of good roads made the task impossible. Instead, Union general Don Carlos Buell and his successor William S. Rosecrans preferred to move on an axis that would take them through Middle Tennessee and then angle southeastward to Chattanooga, which roads, railroads, river, and mountains made the practical gateway not only to East Tennessee but to the Deep South as well. With that approach Lincoln had to be content, but the generals were not moving fast enough to suit him.

Nevertheless, by late summer 1863, he had reason to be satisfied with the military situation. The blockade had tightened up considerably. Vicksburg and an army of 30,000 Rebels had fallen to Grant on July 4, achieving the long-sought goal of opening the Mississippi, and if Union forces in the East were not much closer to Richmond, they at least had dealt *Lee* his first solid tactical defeat – and a fearful bleeding – at the battle of Gettysburg, July 1 – 3. In the center of the country, Rosecrans finally moved against his opponent, Confederate general Braxton *Bragg*, and in a brilliant late June and early July campaign, had forced him completely out of Middle Tennessee and all the way back to Chattanooga.

The series of maneuvers that led directly to the clash of armies near Chickamauga Creek in northwest Georgia began in mid-August. While *Bragg* and his Army of Tennessee sat in Chattanooga, Confederate authorities in Richmond contemplated how they could reinforce him so as to hold that vital rail center and gateway to the Deep South and East Tennessee. Confederate president Jefferson *Davis* and his military advisers even hoped that *Bragg* might perhaps retake the territory that he had lost in Middle Tennessee, regain the military momentum, and give a much-needed boost to sagging Confederate morale.

Rosecrans and his Army of the Cumberland lay a few dozen miles northwest of Chattanooga, on the other side of the rugged Cumberland Mountains. The Washington authorities were not at all content to see Rosecrans rest on the laurels of his nearly bloodless accomplishments that summer. Territory had been gained, but *Bragg's* army had not been destroyed. After the major Federal midsummer victories at Gettysburg and Vicksburg, Union authorities wanted blows struck hard and fast and the rebellion finished off. With the goal of freeing East Tennessee now in sight, Lincoln was more anxious than ever for its realization. Secretary of War Edwin M. Stanton and General in Chief Henry W. Halleck applied constant pressure on Rosecrans for an early advance.

Finally, on August 16, Rosecrans's army moved forward. In a daring maneuver, Rosecrans separated the army's three corps in order to flank *Bragg* and maneuver more rapidly through the few gaps in the towering barrier of Lookout Mountain. The XXI Corps, under Maj. Gen. Thomas L. Crittenden, would threaten Chattanooga directly, then move up the Tennessee River around the point of Lookout (the present route of I-24). The XIV Corps, under Maj. Gen. George H. Thomas, would advance eighteen miles to the south of Crittenden, passing through Steven's Gap. Still farther south would be Maj. Gen. Alexander McCook's XX Corps, advancing through Winston's Gap, fully forty-two miles from Chattanooga and the opposite flank of the Army of the Cumberland.

The plan was a good one, and it worked. With another Union army under Ambrose Burnside simultaneously advancing through Cumberland Gap and toward Knoxville in the heart of East Tennessee, *Bragg* had almost no choice but to take Crittenden's fake seriously. A Federal move upstream on the Tennessee River was simply too dangerous to ignore. When Rosecrans moved downstream instead, he caught *Bragg* badly out of position and turned him, forcing him to retreat rather than run the risk of being trapped in Chattanooga. As Confederate deserters entered Rosecrans's lines, they told tales of utter demoralization, a Confederate army fleeing desperately and about to go to pieces. Elated, Rosecrans continued his advance, his corps still spread out for maximum speed. He was in for a surprise.

Bragg had been outmaneuvered, but he was not ready to give up. He had begun receiving reinforcements from Mississippi, and more were on the way from Virginia. The wily Confederate concentrated his army at La Fayette, Georgia, opposite Steven's Gap, and prepared to strike back. The "deserters" who entered Union lines were in fact spies, dispatched by *Bragg* with the mission of deceiving Rosecrans into keeping his army in its vulnerable deployment. By September 9 *Bragg* was closer to the isolated XIV Corps than it was to either of the other two Union corps. It was an incredible opportunity for the Confederates to crush the Army of the Cumberland piece by piece.

Bragg tried to seize the opportunity, but his subordinate generals failed him. For months trouble had been brewing among the high ranks of the Army of Tennessee. A curious collection of brave and brilliant officers mixed in with misfits and malcontents, sustained by politics despite *Bragg's* efforts to purge the incompetents, the Army of Tennessee's officer corps had convinced itself that *Bragg* was solely to blame for all the Confederacy's many military woes between the Appalachians and the Mississippi. Their mood by now was all but mutinous. On September 9 and 10 Lt. Gen. D. H. *Hill* and Maj. Gen. Thomas C. *Hindman* refused to obey orders that would have led to the destruction of all or part of Thomas's corps. The recalcitrant generals had by this time come to think that any order *Bragg* gave was bound to be disastrously wrong. In this case, *Hindman* took counsel of his fears and became convinced that the enemy was more numerous, better prepared, and far closer to receiving reinforcement than was actually the case.

On September 12 *Bragg's* strategy procured yet another amazing opportunity, this time to destroy Crittenden's XXI Corps, isolated on the Union northern flank. In a virtual replay of the previous incident, however, Lt. Gen. Leonidas *Polk* and Maj. Gen. Simon B. *Buckner* refused their commander's orders, for similar reasons, and the opportunity slipped away.

At this point Rosecrans realized his danger, drew his army together, and began to slide northward, along the west bank of Chickamauga Creek, toward a more secure position in Chattanooga. *Bragg*, on the east bank of the Chickamauga, had one last chance to destroy the Army of the Cumberland.

He hoped to get north of Rosecrans, between the Union army and Chattanooga. Then he planned to attack, pushing the Army of the Cumberland southward into a mountain valley called McLemore's Cove. No good roads led out of the cove, and Rosecrans would never escape with his army if he were once shoved into such a trap. By the evening of September 17 reinforcements had raised *Bragg's* numbers to about 65,000 men. Rosecrans, with only about 62,000, had his left (northern) flank at Lee and Gordon's Mill on Chickamauga Creek (about 3 miles south of the Chickamauga National Battlefield Visitor Center). Much of *Bragg's* army was farther north on the east bank. The next step for the Confederates was to cross the creek and place themselves squarely between Rosecrans and Chattanooga. Only a small screening force–a few brigades of mounted Federals–stood in their way.

On September 18 *Bragg's* Confederates fought their way across the creek, seizing first Reed's Bridge and then Alexander's Bridge further upstream, and closer to Lee and Gordon's Mill. The Union mounted forces, a brigade of cavalry at Reed's Bridge and one of mounted infantry at Alexander's, nevertheless accomplished the most important part of their mission by giving notice to Rosecrans and delaying the Confederates almost all day. The Southerners could advance only a short distance westward from the creek before darkness compelled them to halt.

Before you begin your tour of the Chickamauga battlefield, you may want to make sure you have seen the most important exhibits that the Visitor Center has to offer.

Right: Lee and Gordon's Mill as it looked at the time of the battle. Courtesy National Archives, accession no.111s.b.4791

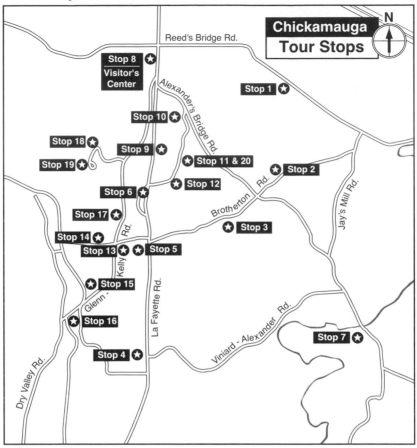

The Chickamauga National Military Park Visitor Center

The Visitor Center is a useful resource for students of the battlefield. Besides displays of Civil War cannon (in front), complete with information on the type and characteristics, it also includes a slide presentation on the history of the Chickamauga National Battlefield Park and a fine Civil War bookstore. Most interesting, perhaps, is the Fuller Gun Collection, which contains several types of weapons used in the battle of Chickamauga. In the first alcove on the right are ordinary Civil War rifles of various makes but the same basic pattern. Such weapons equipped the vast majority of the infantrymen at Chickamauga. In the second alcove on the left is the Spencer Repeating Rifle, which was used with devastating effect by Wilder's brigade. In the fourth (last) alcove on the right is the Colt Revolving Rifle. Though inferior in design to the excellent Spencer, the Colt Revolving Rifle was nevertheless used effectively by several companies of the 21st Ohio in that regiment's epic stand on Horseshoe Ridge. A small museum room beyond the gun collection is also interesting.

Once you have become acquainted with the Visitor Center, you are ready to begin your exploration of the Chickamauga battlefield. First, let's consider the action on September 19, 1863, the first full day of pitched battle.

Optional Excursions

Before visiting the scenes of the September 19 fighting, you may want to visit one or both of the key crossings of Chickamauga Creek, where the Confederates fought their way to the west bank on September 18, making the following two days of battle possible. If so, *turn left* out of the Visitor Center parking lot and *proceed* 0.1 mile to the traffic light at REED'S BRIDGE ROAD. *Turn right. Proceed* 2.6 miles to REED'S BRIDGE. Park in the turnout on the right, just before the bridge. Turn to optional excursion 1, Reed's Bridge.

Overview of the First Day, September 19, 1863

Bragg began the day hoping to drive southwestward, hit the Union flank, and crumple the Army of the Cumberland into McLemore's Cove, cut off from retreat. Rosecrans planned to go on sliding his army sideways—northward—to get between *Bragg* and Chattanooga and keep from being cut off. As both tried simultaneously to carry out their designs in the rolling woodlands between Chickamauga Creek and Missionary Ridge, their armies stumbled into a tangled but vicious moving fight that made up the first day's battle at Chickamauga.

Rosecrans had stolen a march on *Bragg* the night before by sending three divisions of Thomas's XIV Corps marching through the darkness to the Kelly Farm, about three miles to the north of his previous northern flank at Lee and Gordon's Mill. *Bragg* was unaware the next morning as he prepared to launch his attack that now instead of being on the enemy's left flank, he had the enemy on his own right flank. The forces collided shortly after dawn, when Thomas sent a division forward in response to an inaccurate report that only a single Confederate brigade was west of the creek. That advancing Federal division was in fact approaching almost the entire Confederate army, but it was approaching on the Confederate right flank. Patrolling that flank was the cavalry of the redoubtable Nathan Bedford *Forrest*, which absorbed the first shock of the Union advance. *Bragg* shifted infantry to meet this threat. Thomas sent more of his divisions advancing into the woods toward the creek to counter the increased pressure, and Rosecrans shuffled troops northward from the army's positions south of Lee and Gordon's Mill with commendable speed, keeping Thomas at least even with the forces *Bragg* was throwing into the rapidly growing fight.

As the battle grew, it spread southward. The bulk of both armies lay south of the point of initial contact, and as both armies moved up to support their comrades first engaged, the conflict naturally expanded toward them. Throughout the fight, Rosecrans's goal was to retain control of the La Fayette Road, a major north-south route that was his primary (but not only) link with Chattanooga and his line of communication. *Bragg*, his initial plan foiled, wanted to stabilize his own front, firmly locate his enemy, and do him what damage he could.

Around the middle of the day the Federals had the better of the struggle, driving the Confederates back in the Winfrey Field sector, in the north-central part of the battlefield. Elsewhere troops of the two armies seemed to fight each other to a standstill. Especially bloody fighting raged back and forth

The Sinkhole Near the Widow Glen's House. This sinkhole contained the only water to be had in the central part of the battlefield. As the battle progressed, wounded men and horses came to drink. Some of them died here, and their bodies lay in the pool. BLCW 3:656.

across the Viniard Farm and the surrounding woods, at the southern end of the battlefield. Then, late in the afternoon, a gap opened between the Federals fighting at the Viniard Farm and those farther north. Keeping a front closed up was all but impossible when nearly every unit was either engaged or marching and extensive woods made long, panoramic views impossible. The gap, and the advance of yet another Confederate division, Maj. Gen. Alexander P. *Stewart's*, created the crisis of the day for Rosecrans, though at his headquarters at the Widow Glenn's house, he knew little of it until it was over. A major segment of the Union center collapsed in the Brotherton Field, and triumphant Confederates surged forward in pursuit. Yet the crisis passed almost as quickly as it came. Strong reinforcements were already on the way to the threatened sector, and the Confederates who made the breakthrough lacked support. By sundown the front had been stabilized again, and the two armies were fought out for the day – almost.

As the sun dipped toward Missionary Ridge, west of the battlefield, Maj. Gen. Patrick R. *Cleburne's* division, the Army of Tennessee's best, moved up from a position it had been holding on the east bank south of Lee and Gordon's Mill and crossed to the west bank behind *Bragg's* center. By then it was probably too late to accomplish anything in support of *Stewart* and certainly too late to accomplish anything elsewhere, but through a series of poor judgments the division was nevertheless launched in a useless attack. Maj. Gen. St. John R. *Liddell*, commanding another division in that sector, urged corps commander *Polk* to send *Cleburne* in at once. *Liddell* was excited and fresh from the heat of battle and may well have been oblivious to the time of day. *Polk* may have assumed *Liddell* knew what was best on the spot, and *Cleburne* had to obey *Polk's* orders. The result was a confused nighttime battle in the Winfrey Field and surrounding woods. Though it added to the numbers of dead and wounded on both sides and left *Cleburne's* crack division badly ill-deployed for the next day's fighting, it accomplished little else.

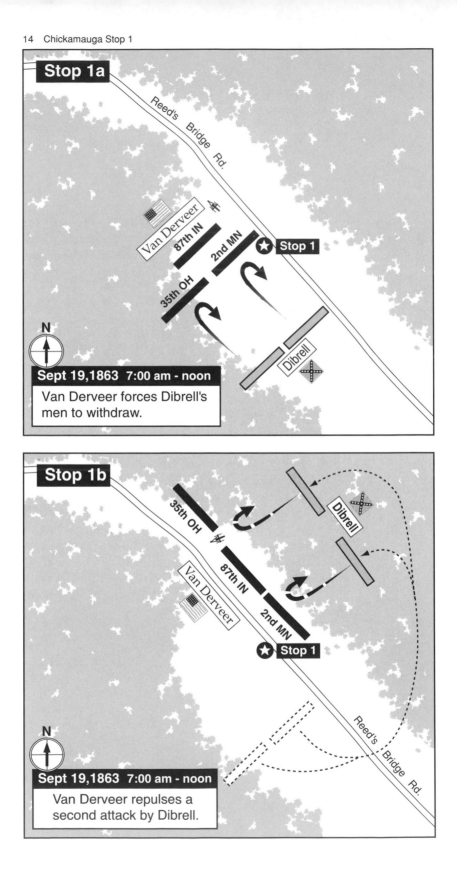

Stop 1a

Reed's Bridge Rd.

Van Derveer

87th IN

2nd MN

Stop 1

35th OH

Dibrell

N

Sept 19,1863 7:00 am - noon

Van Derveer forces Dibrell's men to withdraw.

Stop 1b

35th OH

Dibrell

Van Derveer

87th IN

2nd MN

Stop 1

Reed's Bridge Rd.

N

Sept 19,1863 7:00 am - noon

Van Derveer repulses a second attack by Dibrell.

STOP 1   Reed's Bridge Road   7:00 A.M.

First Blood

Directions

On leaving the Visitor Center parking lot, *turn left* and *proceed* 0.1 mile to the stop light at REED'S BRIDGE ROAD. *Turn right. Proceed* 1.0 mile and park in the curbside parking area on the right. Walk to the tablet for Col. Ferdinand C. Van Derveer's brigade. Stand near the tablet and face in the direction the nearby cannons are pointing (southeast).

Orientation

You are standing on Van Derveer's line of battle on the morning of September 19, when his was the left flank brigade in the advance of Brig. Gen. John M. Brannan's division from Kelly Field into the woods around Reed's Bridge and Jay's Mill. During the first phase of the action the Confederates of *Forrest's* division were advancing directly toward you.

What Happened

Throughout the night of September 18–19, Thomas's XIV Corps marched north up the Chattanooga–La Fayette Road (henceforth called simply La Fayette Road) to prevent the Confederates from getting around to the north of the army. At dawn, Thomas, having arrived with his lead division in the vicinity of Kelly Field, about 1 mile to your right rear (southwest), received a false report that only a single Confederate brigade was west of the creek near Reed's Bridge. He dispatched Brannan's division to advance eastward, toward the creek, and destroy this supposedly isolated Southern brigade. Brannan advanced with his left flank (Van Derveer's brigade) guiding on the Reed's Bridge Road, down which you have just driven, but instead of bagging a lone Confederate brigade, Brannan ran head-on into two brigades of Maj. Gen. Nathan Bedford *Forrest's* cavalry, screening the right of *Bragg's* army. Brannan drove them back and finally halted with his line facing east, running southward from here, its right flank, at the far end of the line, about 100 yards short of the Brotherton Road, in deep woods a few hundred yards from Chickamauga Creek.

Forrest called for infantry support, received two brigades of Maj. Gen. William H. T. *Walker's* corps, and immediately hurled them into the fight. Brannan's right flank brigade, that of Col. John T. Croxton, broke under a powerful flanking attack by Brig. Gen. Claudius C. *Wilson's* brigade, but here on the Union left, Van Derveer's brigade performed the first of its several remarkable services during this battle. First it repulsed two brigades of *Forrest's* dismounted cavalry. Then it did the same to *Wilson's* infantry brigade as it attempted to follow up its success over Croxton.

After repulsing Confederates advancing directly toward this position, Van Derveer detected that other Confederates were swinging wide through the woods around his left to come in from across the road on his left rear. These were the cavalrymen of George G. *Dibrell's* brigade of *Forrest's* division, fighting like infantry. There was little time to spare. Van Derveer faced his brigade to the rear, marched them across the road, and swung them onto a line roughly parallel to the road, taking advantage of a gentle rise in the ground. The Confederates came into view about 100 yards from the road, advancing up the slope. Van Derveer's men opened fire, surprising the Confederates who had thought to surprise them. Faced with alert and resolute infantry in a strong position, *Dibrell's* tired troopers were forced to withdraw.

Analysis

In the seesaw fighting that raged through the woods from this point south during the morning of September 19, units of each side were frequently routed when an enemy line, whether by accident or design, approached one of their flanks. In these thick woods, where visibility was anywhere from 50 to 150 yards, a commander had to be exceptionally alert to be able to perceive enemy movements and react before it was too late. Van Derveer's alertness and the ability of his brigade to perform tough maneuvers in battle canceled the advantage the Confederates might have won from *Dibrell's* enterprise and intelligence and his men's courage and endurance.

Further Reading

Cozzens, *This Terrible Sound*, 135–36, 147–49.

Optional Excursion

To view the other flank of Brannan's division, where it was struck by *Wilson's* Confederates, *proceed* in the direction you were just traveling 0.9 mile to JAY'S MILL ROAD. *Turn right. Proceed* 0.1 mile to BROTHERTON ROAD. *Turn right. Proceed* about 0.3 mile and park in the turnout on the left near the sign pointing toward "Bragg's Headquarters." Turn to optional excursion 3, Woods West of Jay's Mill. Note: This was a headquarters site for *Bragg* on the second day of the battle, not during the fighting being discussed here.

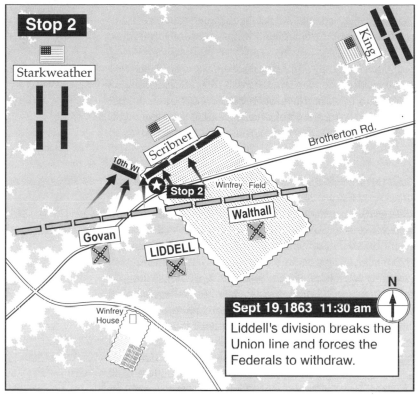

Stop 2

Starkweather

King

Scribner

Brotherton Rd.

10th WI

Stop 2   Winfrey Field

Walthall

Govan

LIDDELL

N

Winfrey House

Sept 19,1863 11:30 am

Liddell's division breaks the Union line and forces the Federals to withdraw.

STOP 2   Winfrey Field   11:30 A.M.

Attack and Counterattack

Directions

Proceed in the direction you were just traveling on REED'S BRIDGE ROAD not quite 0.9 mile to JAY'S MILL ROAD. *Turn right. Proceed* a little over 0.1 mile to BROTHERTON ROAD. *Bear right. Proceed* 0.4 mile to Winfrey Field. Park in the unimproved turnout on the right just before leaving the field. Stand on the top of the embankment beside the road near the edge of the woods. Face east, back toward the direction from which you have just driven, along the line of Brotherton Road.

Orientation

The field in front of you was, at the time of the battle, covered with weeds and dead cornstalks. Brig. Gen. Absalom Baird's Union division was on your left, its right brigade, commanded by Col. Benjamin F. Scribner, along the tree line on the left side of the field. At the far end of Baird's line, his left brigade, under Brig. Gen. John H. King, was positioned about 600 yards farther into the woods north of here, your left front. Baird had one brigade, commanded by Brig. Gen. John Starkweather, in reserve, about 500 yards to your left.

Liddell's Confederate division attacked from your right and right rear. Note that most of the monuments in Winfrey Field represent action later in the day.

What Happened

As fighting grew hotter in the woods between Kelly Field and Chickamauga Creek, Thomas sent Baird's division to come up and support Brannan on his right. Baird pushed back *Wilson's* and *Forrest's* Confederates that had driven in Brannan's right flank. Baird halted with his own right flank near here, deployed as described above.

Then it was *Bragg's* turn to up the ante, sending in the two-brigade division of Maj. Gen. St. John R. *Liddell*. Brig. Gen. Edward C. *Walthall's* Mississippi brigade formed *Liddell's* right, advancing across the field in front of you, roughly from your right to your left. Col. Daniel *Govan's* Arkansas brigade advanced entirely through the woods behind you.

Govan struck Scribner's right flank. Scribner pulled his right regiment, the 10th Wisconsin, back at right angles, but it was no use. *Govan's* men poured around the newly extended right and at the same time crushed the hinge of the line, about at the corner of the field to your left. The 10th Wisconsin disintegrated. Meanwhile, *Walthall's* Mississippians, after lying down to catch their breath in the vicinity of Brotherton Road (in front of you), charged Scribner's line along the rail fence and sent the Federals reeling. *Liddell's* division continued its advance, routing Starkweather and King in succession before being counterattacked by elements of Brannan's division, who had rested and refilled their cartridge boxes since the action described at stop 1.

Later in the day, Brig Gen. Richard W. Johnson's Union division, attacking from the southwest, drove the Confederates back to this position and held the line of the rail fence on the left side of the field until withdrawing to Kelly Field after dark (see optional excursion 5).

Analysis

Several factors aided *Liddell* in wrecking Baird's larger division. Some of Scribner's men complained after the battle that their position was faulty. They preferred to load and fire lying down, a difficult task with muzzle-loaders. The soldier had to roll onto his back and hold the muzzle of his rifle at arm's length above him, which was impossible when, as was the case for Scribner's men here, the troops were lying on a downhill slope, their heads lower than their feet. The men of the 10th Wisconsin had to stand up to reload after their first volley, and it was at that moment that the regiment broke for the rear.

Another aspect of Scribner's faulty position was that a

wooded ravine, about 90 yards behind you and roughly parallel to the edge of the field near which you now stand, provided cover for *Govan's* charging Arkansans just 50 yards from the positions of the 10th Wisconsin.

Liddell's other brigade, *Walthall's*, seems to have been especially effective in this fight for the ironic reason that it had been issued the wrong ammunition, greatly reducing the effectiveness of its rifles, particularly if it should become engaged in a lengthy firefight. In response, *Walthall* had his troops cover the last 100 yards from Brotherton Road to the Union line in a single rush, without pausing. This was a tactic that proved successful on several occasions in the Civil War and that some modern students of the war believe could have achieved good combat results without the slaughter customary to Civil War battles. Yet men with perfectly good rifles were loath to perform it. *Walthall* had that problem solved for him. He was also aided by the weeds, dead cornstalks, and slight contour of the ground that covered his men while they caught their breath lying along Brotherton Road.

The most important reason for *Liddell's* success was his fortuitous approach directly on the flank of Baird's entire division in wooded country that kept Baird and his subordinates from reacting until it was too late. Each of Baird's brigades was taken in flank one after the other and was defeated fighting alone against *Liddell's* full division.

Vignette

Years later, Colonel Scribner eloquently described the mind-numbing rush of battle as his brigade went to pieces under *Liddell's* attack: "It seemed as though a terrible cyclone was sweeping over the earth, driving everything before it. All things appeared to be rushing by me in horizontal lines, all parallel to each other. The missiles of the enemy whistling and whirring by, seemed to draw the elements in the same lines of motion, sound, light and air uniting in the rush."

Further Reading

Cozzens, *This Terrible Sound*, 141–51, 186–95; Tucker, *Chickamauga*, 133–37.

Optional Excursion

If you would like to explore the ground over which *Govan's* and *Walthall's* Confederates defeated King's brigade and were subsequently driven back by Brannan's division, you can do so by making a 0.6-mile hike. First, *drive back* the way you came just over 0.4 mile to the sign for "Bragg's Headquarters" and the nearby trailhead signs. Park and take the red-blazed trail on the left-hand side of the road (relative to the direction you were just driving). Turn to optional excursion 4, Woods West of Jay's Mill. Note: When returning to the main tour, bear in mind that the instructions at the end of optional excursion 4 will direct you back to stop 2. Since you have already covered that stop, simply return to it (turning around and driving back the way you came) and then follow the directions at the beginning of stop 3.

Confederate line of battle in the Chickamauga Woods. BLCW 3:638

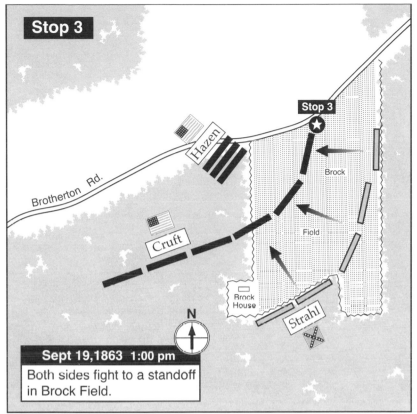

Stop 3

Hazen

Brotherton Rd.

Stop 3

Brock

Cruft

Field

Brock House

Strahl

N

Sept 19,1863 1:00 pm

Both sides fight to a standoff
in Brock Field.

STOP 3   Brock Field   1:00 P.M.

Standoff

Directions   *Proceed* about 0.5 mile to Brock Field. *En route* you will cross
an intersection about 0.2 mile from Winfrey Field. As you do,
look to your right front. The undergrowth at this point has
been cleared and it gives a glimpse of the battlefield vegeta-
tion as it was in 1863. Arriving at Brock Field, park in the second turnout on the left, near the "pointing hand" sign for
"Brock Field." Walk back along the road a few yards to the
highest ground on the edge of the field, under the large cedar tree. Face the prominent monument near the far end of
the field.

Orientation   You are standing near the left flank of Brig. Gen. William B.
Hazen's line, facing along the line toward the center of his
brigade. The two larger monuments in the field commemorate Hazen's regiments. The one on the left is to the 124th
Ohio, that on the right is to the 41st Ohio. The Union brigades

of Brig. Gen. Charles Cruft and Col. William Grose were in the woods beyond the far edge of the field on your right front. These three brigades made up the division of Maj. Gen. John M. Palmer. The Confederate brigades of Brig. Gen. Preston *Smith* and Brig. Gen. Otho F. *Strahl*, of Maj. Gen. Benjamin F. *Cheatham's* division, advanced from the woods on your left front.

What Happened

Even as combat continued to rage in Winfrey Field and sur- rounding woodlands to your left rear (northeast of your pre- sent position), the fighting spread rapidly southwestward as both generals fed additional units into the battle. As John- son's division advanced to rectify the situation around the Winfrey Field, Rosecrans sent Palmer's division in on John- son's right, suggesting that Palmer advance *en échelon* to the right—that is, with his center brigade (Cruft) to the right of and 100 yards behind his left brigade (Hazen) and with his right brigade (Grose) still further right and another 100 yards behind Cruft. As *Cheatham's* Confederates advanced from the southwest, Palmer's division could easily swing to the right and into line, forming a rough arc that faced from east (on Hazen's left—here) to south (on Grose's right). Thus Palmer avoided the fate that befell Baird.

What occurred here in Brock Field was a straightforward, stand-up slugging match between Hazen's Federals (occa- sionally spelled by other Union troops long enough to draw ammunition) and *Smith's* and *Strahl's* Confederates. The op- posing forces reached the field from opposite sides at about the same time, and the battle was a furious firefight, with Hazen's regiments twice emptying their cartridge boxes (at 40 to 80 rounds per man each time). By 3:00 P.M. both sides were pretty well fought out, and a lull ensued in this sector.

In the woods about half a mile to your right front, the bri- gade of Brig. Gen. Marcus *Wright* (also of *Cheatham's* division) advanced. *Wright* mistakenly believed he was coming up to support other Confederate units already engaged. Instead, he blundered head-on into the waiting brigades of Cruft and Grose, who easily threw back his confused assault.

Analysis

Rosecrans's suggestion that Palmer advance *en échelon* indi- cates that he apparently understood the cause of the defeat of Baird's and—earlier and to a lesser extent—Brannan's divi- sions during the morning hours. That was no mean feat in the confusion of a rapidly developing battle and in this heav- ily wooded country. Rosecrans has received little credit for his conduct of the battle of Chickamauga, but he deserves credit for this stage of the fight.

With nobody flanking anybody else, and with this large open field to allow troops to use—at times—almost the full 400-yard effective range of their rifles, this fight took a form more familiar on Civil War battlefields, a bloody deadlock in which neither side gained a clear advantage. In the woods, *Wright's* disadvantage in numbers and mistake about his position decided the contest almost before it began. *Wright's* confusion is understandable because the woods in that area were apparently some of the thickest on the battlefield. A Federal officer complained that visibility was as little as 50 yards, while *Wright's* men first perceived the presence of the enemy in their front at a range of about 100 yards. *Wright's* artillery battery had great difficulty in getting through the woods—more, it seems, than was encountered by batteries operating further north.

Vignette

In the opening minutes of the fighting here in Brock Field, Company B, 124th Ohio, was deployed as skirmishers. These Buckeyes were going into battle for the first time, though they had been in the army nearly ten months. Corp. William Atkins was firing his first shots in earnest. A schoolteacher in peacetime life, Atkins knew why he was crouching in northwest Georgia shooting at other men across a hardscrabble cornfield. A strong abolitionist, Atkins had enlisted to strike a blow against slavery. Now he had his chance, and he loaded and fired avidly. A bullet struck him in the left shoulder. Beside him, Capt. George Lewis looked in horror at the ugly wound and ordered Atkins to the rear for treatment. "See captain," the corporal replied, "I am not much hurt, I want to give them another." Despite his wound, Atkins managed to reload his rifle, but before he could fire again, another bullet struck him full in the chest, killing him instantly.

Further Reading

Cozzens, *This Terrible Sound*, 154–66; Tucker, *Chickamauga*, 144–47; Woodworth, *A Deep Steady Thunder*, 39–41.

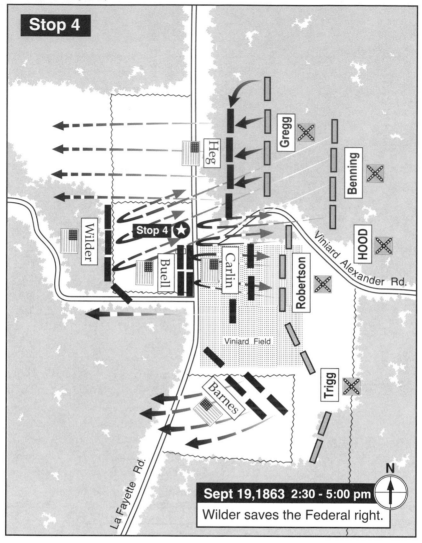

Stop 4

Sept 19,1863 2:30 - 5:00 pm

Wilder saves the Federal right.

STOP 4

Viniard Field   2:30–5:00 P.M.

Wilder Saves the Union Right

Directions

Proceed straight ahead about 0.7 mile to LA FAYETTE ROAD. *Turn left. Proceed* not quite 1.0 mile to Viniard Field. Park in the parking area on the right. Stand on the grass at the further edge of the parking area, near the sign pointing toward the Heg Monument, 200 feet away. Face south, the direction in which you were just driving.

Orientation

Union troops advanced from right to left across La Fayette Road, their line stretching about 400 yards both in front of and behind you, both in the woods and in the open Viniard Field (where you now see several monuments to your left front). The line of trees and brush to the right of the road, much less extensive in 1863, marked the course of a shallow gully or dry streambed that is still present (you can see a small, modern footbridge over this stream–no longer dry–about 75 yards directly to your right). In front of you, between road and ditch, were the buildings and fences of Viniard Farm (marked by a Park Service tablet on the other side of the thicket). Beyond the ditch on your right, the field continues another 300 yards to the point where the forest begins again. Along that far tree line (just visible through a gap in the trees to your right), Col. John T. Wilder's brigade of mounted infantry, armed with Spencer Repeating Rifles, had taken position and thrown up rough breastworks.

What Happened   By early afternoon the fighting had become general all along the front. It next grew intense here, where some of the fiercest and bloodiest combat of the first day took place. About 2:30 that afternoon each commanding general decided to try turning the other's southern flank. For this purpose XXI Corps commander Crittenden led the divisions of Brig. Gen. Jefferson C. Davis and Brig. Gen. Thomas J. Wood and one brigade of the division of Brig. Gen. Horatio P. Van Cleve, plus Wilder's men. These units were not all of his corps, simply a hodgepodge of troops Rosecrans had made available to him for the mission. Command arrangements among their various officers and Crittenden were clumsy at best, but Rosecrans was performing the difficult task of shuffling his army sideways while in contact with the enemy, and he used whatever units were handy when need arose.

For the Confederates, Maj. Gen. John B. *Hood* commanded the divisions of Bushrod *Johnson* and Brig. Gen. Evander M. *Law* and one brigade of the division of Brig. Gen. William *Preston*.

Crittenden's troops moved out from La Fayette Road, past where you now stand. *Hood's* men advanced from the east, and a desperate fight ensued for control of the vital La Fayette Road. Each side charged repeatedly, only to be pushed back. The Federals were finally driven across La Fayette Road through the Viniard farmyard (where many were shot down trying to climb a fence) and into the gully beyond. From that position fragments of the various Federal brigades resisted further Confederate attempts to advance, and there Brig. Gen. Hans C. Heg was mortally wounded trying to rally his men (near the spot marked by the pyramid of cannonballs to your right). Three successive Confederate flanking movements were wrecked by Wilder, who swung his brigade outward from its position in the tree line (on your far right) to points where it was most needed, using the firepower of his Spencers to check each Confederate advance. Finally, direct Confederate pressure broke Union resistance in the gully, and the troops there streamed back through Wilder's position. Confederates followed up the success but got no farther than the gully, where once again Wilder's firepower proved overwhelming. As the Southerners hunkered down to try to hold the ditch, Wilder moved his attached battery of artillery forward to a position on your right rear, so as to sweep the length of the gully with canister, sending the Confederates fleeing back in this direction, across La Fayette Road.

As evening came on, the division of Maj. Gen. Philip Sheridan came up, and its lead brigade became involved in the fighting before darkness closed this bloody segment of the battle with the Federal right flank battered but still intact and the forces in this sector, with the possible exception of Sheridan's and Wilder's, having fought themselves to exhaustion.

Analysis

The woods for 200 or 300 yards just east of La Fayette Road from here northward to Brotherton Road were some of the thickest on the battlefield, including dense undergrowth of blackjack (scrub) oak that limited visibility in some places to as little as 20 yards. This had contributed to the confusion and defeat of *Wright's* brigade of *Cheatham's* division further north (see stop 3). Here it favored the Confederates, as Crittenden's forces left a gap on their left (behind you; you'll discover more of the results of this at the next stop). Southerners advancing through the woods moved through this gap and flanked the Federal line here.

The downfall of Confederate efforts in this sector was provided by Wilder's brigade and its rapid-firing Spencers. A brigade of ordinary, "leg" infantry until just a few months before, Wilder's command, nicknamed the Lightning Brigade, had been mounted as part of Rosecrans's efforts to give the army a more powerful cavalry force. The men had been eager to have the new seven-shot Spencer repeaters and had been willing to purchase the rifles with their own money if necessary. Before it came to that, the government had equipped them with these formidable weapons. With the same range and lethality as ordinary rifle-muskets, the Spencers had seven to ten times the rate of fire (up to 20 rounds per minute), making Wilder's brigade equivalent in firepower to two and a half divisions of conventionally equipped troops (i.e., the entire Confederate force engaged on this part of the field).

Vignette

When Wilder's artillery began to blast double and triple loads of canister along the length of the ditch packed with Rebels, the colonel himself admitted, "It actually seemed a pity to kill men so. They fell in heaps; and I had it in my heart to order the firing to cease, to end the awful sight."

Further Reading

Cozzens, *This Terrible Sound*, 196–229; Tucker, *Chickamauga*, 162–75; Woodworth, *A Deep Steady Thunder*, 45–52.

Further Exploration

If time permits, you may want to view Lee and Gordon's Mill, which marked Rosecrans's right (southern) flank on the morning of September 19. *Proceed* southward another 1.5 miles to LEE GORDON MILL ROAD (at stoplight). *Turn left. Proceed* 0.2 mile to a stop sign and *turn right. Proceed* 0.1 mile to Chickamauga Creek. Before crossing the creek, pull over to the shoulder and stop. The mill is the old building to your left front. The Federal markers near the mill refer to units that were here (but not engaged) on September 19, while the Confederate markers refer to units that were here (but also not engaged) on the twentieth.

You may also want to visit the Gordon-Lee Mansion, Rosecrans's headquarters on September 18 and a makeshift hospital during and after the battle: From Lee and Gordon's Mill, *turn around and go back* the way you were just driving. *Proceed straight ahead* through the intersection of LEE GORDON MILL ROAD and LA FAYETTE ROAD. At the next traffic signal you come to, *turn left. Proceed* to the traffic signal in the downtown section of the town of Chickamauga (Crawfish Springs in 1863). At that signal, *turn left.* The Gordon-Lee Mansion is the fourth building on your right, a large brick structure with imposing pillars in front, at 217 Cove Road. You may view it from the road (it is on private property).

Built in 1847, the Gordon-Lee Mansion is now a National Historic Site and a bed-and-breakfast, in which one can sleep where Rosecrans slept and view an interesting one-room museum exhibit on the second floor. All of the interiors are completely furnished with period items (except for modern plumbing conveniences unknown to Americans of the 1860s).

Retrace your route to stop 4 and then follow the directions for stop 5.

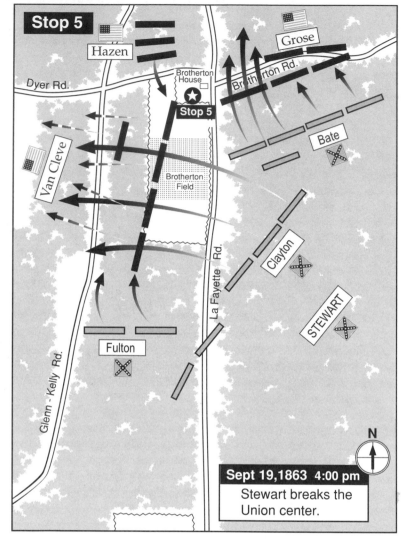

STOP 5   Brotherton Field   4:00 P.M.

Stewart Breaks the Union Center

Directions   *Turn around and proceed* north (back the way you came) 1.0 mile to the curbside parking area in front of the Brotherton House. *Turn left* into the lot and park. Walk up the path that leads around the back of the house and then across the grass past the end of the rail fence to the Park Service tablet for Hazen's brigade, the second of the tablets you see strung out along the ridge. The cannon you pass belonged to *Bledsoe's* Missouri Battery and were used in action on the second day. For now, try to ignore them.

Orientation   Face east, toward La Fayette Road. The Brotherton House is to your left front. You are standing on a grassy ridge running parallel to La Fayette Road down the middle of Brotherton Field. By midafternoon the Federal line ran along the crest of this ridge. The Confederates advanced out of the woods across the road, less than 100 yards in front of you.

What Happened   When elements of *Johnson's* division struck the gap between Crittenden's forces and those defending this part of the Union line, it created problems for the Federals in both directions. For Crittenden it almost brought disaster around the Viniard Field (stop 4). Here it had equally bad effects. John S. *Fulton's* brigade hit La Fayette Road about 600 yards to your right, flanking the Federal defenders just this side of the gap, driving them out of the woods in front of you and back onto this ridge in some disorder. About 3:30 P.M. the front was stabilized here, with the battered and partially disorganized remnants of Van Cleve's division, along with 20 pieces of artillery, drawn up along the ridge and Palmer's and Joseph J. Reynolds's divisions holding a line that ran along Brotherton Road (which enters La Fayette Road opposite the Brotherton House). Those two divisions faced southeast.

At 3:45 disaster struck the Federals in this position as *Johnson* resumed his flanking attack from the south, reaching the far tree line on your right, while Maj. Gen. A. P. *Stewart's* Confederate division struck Van Cleve's and Palmer's lines here and along Brotherton Road, coming straight out of the woods in front of you, across La Fayette Road, and directly toward the ridgetop line. The Union defense collapsed. *Stewart's* and *Johnson's* Confederates captured two of the guns deployed in the field; the others limbered up and made their escape as best they could, following their fleeing infantry supports. Hazen's brigade made a brief stand near here but was quickly overwhelmed. Brig. Gen. Henry D. *Clayton's* brigade of *Stewart's* division pursued through Brotherton Woods, behind you, while most of Brig. Gen. William B. *Bate's* brigade of the same division went northward, through the adjoining woods north of Dyer Road, on your left, threatening to roll up the entire Federal line.

Analysis   Several factors contributed to the Confederate success here. 1. The 600-yard gap between the Federals at the south end of this field, on your right, and those around Viniard Field allowed Col. John S. *Fulton's* brigade of *Johnson's* division to flank the Union line here in Brotherton Field. Why did the gap exist? The woods made it difficult for a general to survey the battlefield, and the struggle around Viniard Field sucked up some of the Federal reinforcements moving up from Lee and Gordon's Mill that might have closed the gap.

2. After three and a half hours of fighting, Palmer's brigades, which held the line along Brotherton Road, were exhausted and nearly out of ammunition (see stop 3).

3. The woods across La Fayette Road from you were some of the thickest on the battlefield in 1863, probably about as thick as they are today. Visibility was reported to be less than 20 yards (this belt of thickets seemed to extend along the west side of La Fayette Road from here down to Viniard Field [stop 4]). That factor had worked against the Confederates when *Wright's* brigade blundered against Palmer's line (Grose's brigade) earlier in the day (stop 4). Now with *Stewart's* brigades advancing correctly, the thick woods gave the Federals little chance to defend themselves; the attackers were upon them almost as soon as they came in view.

Brotherton Field was a hard place to defend. The natural place to defend a ridge is partway down the front slope. Here that would put the defenders too close to the thick woods across the road for them to use their rifles effectively, much less their artillery. Placing a line along the crest of the ridge (here) gives only a slightly larger field of fire and silhouettes the defenders as perfect targets, while giving the attackers cover under the brow of the slope. To test this, walk about 25 paces forward until you are even with the large, pointed-topped monument to the 9th Indiana. Note that as you walk, you can just begin to see the top of a Park Service tablet commemorating some of the Confederate troops who fought here. It was completely hidden from your previous position. Retiring into the tree line behind you is a little better but still allows defensive fire only after the attackers reach the ridgetop, at a range of about 50 to 100 yards. To make matters worse, a wooded ravine just beyond the south end of the field provides cover for infantrymen picking off artillerists in the open field–an advantage of which *Fulton's* men were quick to avail themselves. Yet Rosecrans was determined to hold La Fayette Road, and once Van Cleve was flanked out of the woods in front of you (to the west), that meant holding Brotherton Field.

Vignette   William B. *Bate*, brigade commander in *Stewart's* division, was known for his hard-driving aggressiveness. Three and a half weeks after the battle, Confederate president Jefferson *Davis* toured the battlefield with Southern officers. In this sector he came to a dead horse that obviously had belonged to a general officer and asked whose it was. The officers informed him it had been *Bate's*. About 300 yards farther he encountered another dead horse, also *Bate's*. A third carcass, that of a "mouse-colored, bobtailed artillery horse," excited the president's curiosity. Informed that *Bate* had been riding the animal when it was shot down, *Davis* was deeply impressed with the Tennesseean's daring. Returning to Richmond not long after, the president appointed *Bate* a major general, though he had been the junior brigadier in the Army of Tennessee.

Further Reading   Cozzens, *This Terrible Sound*, 241–56; Tucker, *Chickamauga*, 148–63; Woodworth, *A Deep Steady Thunder*, 52–57.

Further Exploration   If you have time, you may wish to see where *Clayton's* brigade was stopped, just the other side of Brotherton Woods. If so, *turn right* (south) out of the parking area onto LA FAYETTE ROAD and *proceed* 1.1 miles to GLENN-VINIARD ROAD. *Turn right. Proceed* about 1.5 miles (during which the road changes names to GLENN-KELLY ROAD as it goes around a bend) to the small sign on your left for "Tanyard." *Clayton's* men had, by the time they reached this point, lost all organization. By the time *Clayton* and his officers could get them back under control, Federal units were approaching both from the hilltop beyond the "Tanyard" sign and from in front of you down Glenn-Kelly Road. *Clayton* thought it best to withdraw.

On the Skirmish Line. BLCW 3:31

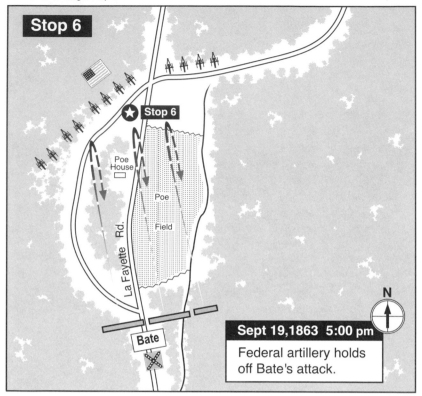

STOP 6

Poe Field   5:00 P.M.

Triumph of the Federal Artillery

Directions

Upon leaving the parking area, *return north* up LA FAYETTE ROAD. *Proceed* 0.4 mile to POE ROAD. *Turn left. Proceed* about 20 yards to the monument and cannons representing Battery M, 4th U.S. Artillery. Park in the turnout here. Then walk back to the "Poe Road" sign near the intersection. Face south, toward the open field, specifically, toward the tall monument (the Georgia Monument) at the other end of the field.

Orientation

La Fayette Road is on your left. On the other side of it are the guns of Battery H, 4th U.S. Artillery. To your right, near where you parked, are those of Battery M of the same regiment, which also took part in this action. The guns at the far end of the field represent units that fought over this ground the next day. In the action we are now considering, *Bate's* brigade, in line of battle, emerged from the far tree line, about 350 yards from where you now stand, advancing directly toward you. His line extended the width of the field, across La Fayette Road, and into the woods to the right of the road.

Anxious to check the potentially disastrous Confederate breakthrough from Brotherton Field, Brig. Gen. William B. Hazen left his brigade and galloped north to try to form a second line of resistance. Here, on the northern edge of Poe Field, he succeeded. Staff members and other mounted officers herded fleeing soldiers into the semblance of a line of battle, cobbled together from fragments of half a dozen regiments. More important, Hazen managed to assemble some 20 pieces of artillery from Batteries H and M, 4th U.S., and Batteries B and F, 1st Ohio, all from Palmer's division, of which Hazen's command was a part. Flushed with their victory over the Federals around the Brotherton House, the Rebels charged aggressively into the field. Hazen's cannon opened fire at once and with devastating effect. *Bate* lost 30 percent of his remaining numbers in little more than three minutes of action. All of his regimental commanders were wounded, and he was forced to retreat back across Brotherton and La Fayette Roads.

Analysis Why did the artillery wreck *Bate's* brigade here while at Brotherton Field an equally numerous line of guns, including some of the same units (for example, Battery H, 4th U.S.), failed to stop the assault there? Hazen's flanks were secure, at least for the moment, and *Bate's* aggressive pursuit had outrun any possible Confederate support. The confusion and hard fighting that had led Rosecrans to leave a 600-yard gap in his line south of Brotherton Field had also kept *Bragg* from having adequate reserves handy to follow up this breakthrough.

Most important, however, was terrain. Poe Field is a large, open, relatively flat area—ideal for the use of Civil War artillery's most effective ammunition: canister. The far edge of the field, 350 yards away, is just comfortably inside effective canister range. To endeavor to cross this field in the face of numerous, well-served cannon with secure flanks was well nigh suicidal, but *Bate* hoped he had the Federals on the run and wanted to maintain momentum. This time the gamble did not pay off.

Vignette Future journalist and short-story writer Ambrose Bierce was on this day an officer of Hazen's staff. He recorded his impressions as the Union cannons opened fire: "For perhaps five minutes—it seemed an hour—nothing could be heard but the infernal din of their discharge and nothing seen through the smoke but a great ascension of dust from the smitten soil. When all was over, and the dust cloud had lifted, the spectacle was too dreadful to describe. The Confederates were still there—all of them, it seemed—some almost under the muzzles of guns. But not a man of all these brave fellows was on his feet, and so thickly were all covered with dust that they looked as if they had been re-clothed in yellow." (Note: Canister is most effective when aimed to strike the ground just in front of the enemy and skip upward into his ranks; thus the dust.)

Further Reading   Cozzens, *This Terrible Sound*, 255–57; Woodworth, *A Deep Steady Thunder*, 54–57.

Optional Excursion   If you have time and interest, you may wish to return to Winfrey Field to examine the ground over which Patrick R. *Cleburne's* Confederate division made a late evening attack on the Union division of Richard W. Johnson. If so, *proceed* 0.2 mile to LA FAYETTE ROAD. *Turn right. Proceed* 0.2 mile to BROTHERTON ROAD. *Turn left. Proceed* 1.3 miles to Winfrey Field. Pull off to the shoulder and park. Walk to the left (relative to the direction you have just been driving) along the edge of the field to the Baldwin Monument, another cannonball pyramid. Turn to optional excursion 5, Winfrey Field.

Feeling the Enemy (detail). BLCW 3:224

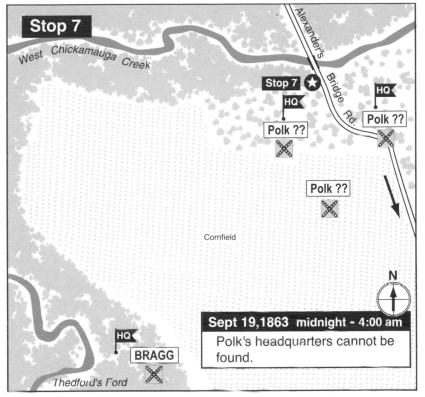

Stop 7

West Chickamauga Creek

Alexander's

Stop 7 ★

HQ

Bridge Rd.

HQ

Polk ??

Polk ??

Polk ??

Cornfield

N

Sept 19,1863 midnight - 4:00 am
Polk's headquarters cannot be
found.

HQ

BRAGG

Thedford's Ford

STOP 7   Alexander's Bridge   midnight to 4:00 A.M.

Missed Connections

Directions   *Proceed straight ahead* about 0.3 mile on POE ROAD to LA FAYETTE
                     ROAD. *Turn right. Proceed* not quite 0.2 mile to BROTHERTON
                     ROAD. *Turn left. Proceed* not quite 1.0 mile to ALEXANDER'S
                     BRIDGE ROAD. *Turn right. Proceed* past the intersections of JAY'S
                     MILL and VINIARD-ALEXANDER roads, a total of 1.4 miles, to
                     Alexander's Bridge. Park in the paved turnout on the right
                     before you reach the bridge. Walk across the bridge and
                     stand on the far side, facing down the road in the direction
                     you were just walking.

Orientation   Behind you is Alexander's Bridge over Chickamauga Creek.
                     In front of you Alexander's Bridge Road, as it did in 1863,
                     winds generally eastward through a mixture of fields, open
                     woods, and cedar breaks.

What Happened   After dark on September 19, as the last scattered shots of *Cle-
                     burne's* night attack sputtered out more than a mile and a
                     half directly behind you (northwest), the top Confederate

generals began to arrive at *Bragg's* first-day headquarters at Thedford's Ford, upstream around a bend of the creek, about 1,100 yards to your right (southwest) as the crow flies but some 3 miles from here by the roads.

Bragg had summoned the officers to plan the next day's action. He was determined to renew the attack. Coming in that night were two more brigades from Virginia along with Lt. Gen. James *Longstreet*, and *Bragg* reorganized his army to give *Longstreet* an important command. The newcomer was to lead a wing of the army, five divisions, while *Polk* would be moved up from his corps command to direct the other wing, also five divisions. *Polk's* wing would be on the Confederate right, *Longstreet's* on the left, and *Polk* was to open the fighting at "day-dawn" on the twentieth, the rest of the army taking up the attack thereafter, each division launching its assault as soon as its neighbor on the right became engaged.

The conference broke up around ten o'clock. An hour later *Polk* arrived somewhere near here, where he had established his headquarters. Accounts vary as to just where it was. One officer recalled its being in the woods on the right of the road less than 50 yards from the bridge. A trooper of *Polk's* escort thought it was in a cedar thicket on the left of the road 100 yards beyond the bridge. As you can see by looking to your left front, a large number of cedars still grow there today. A courier on *Polk's* staff (whose account historian Thomas L. Connelly found the most plausible) remembered the headquarters being between one-half and three-fourths of a mile beyond the bridge and located 100 yards up a small side trail that came into the road.

On the way here, *Polk* had sent a staff officer to *Hill*, whose corps was to launch the "day-dawn" assault, and told him he wanted to see *Hill* at his headquarters. *Hill* meanwhile had gone looking for *Bragg* and later claimed to have been at Thedford's Ford and found no one. By the time he would have been there, after midnight, *Bragg* had turned in for the night, but how *Hill* could have missed headquarters is a mystery except that it was dark in the woods and a damp nighttime mist was rising to mingle with the lingering powder smoke. *Hill* might not have been where he thought he was. At any rate, the staff officer found him and delivered *Polk's* message, but *Hill*, as he later explained, "was much exhausted, having been in the saddle from dawn till midnight, and therefore resolved to rest until three o'clock."

Meanwhile, Polk, anticipating *Hill's* arrival and some difficulty in his finding headquarters, posted a courier here, probably very near where you now are, to keep a fire burning "for an hour or so" and be ready to direct *Hill*. That was about midnight. Another courier was assigned to another fire where the trail to *Polk's* headquarters branched off from Alexander's Bridge road, wherever that was. Around 2:00 A.M. someone at *Polk's* headquarters–the general was asleep by then–told both couriers to leave their posts and turn in. When *Hill* arrived here at the bridge sometime after three o'clock, he could not find *Polk* and so made his way to his lines without having learned anything of the attack his troops were supposed to launch less than three hours hence.

While *Bragg* held his conference at Thedford's Ford, Rosecrans and his corps commanders met at the Widow Glenn's house and agreed to stay on the field for another day of fighting but to strengthen Thomas's position on the left while pulling the right in and back. In effect, the army would be contracting and sliding to the left. Viniard Field, held at enormous cost in blood just a few hours earlier, would now be abandoned. The Union right would then rest on Widow Glenn's Hill, and Rosecrans would, early the next morning, move his headquarters from the Widow Glenn's house to an open knoll overlooking Dyer Field several hundred yards to the north.

Analysis

Much of the explanation for the Confederate command failure is obvious–the darkness, foliage, mist, and powder smoke and the fatigue of everyone involved. Additionally, *Polk* was not a good officer, and failing to see that his orders were carried out was all too typical of him. *Hill* could be inconsistent. That trait had prompted *Lee* to purge him from the Army of Northern Virginia the previous year. *Hill* also seems to have resented the reorganization of the army by *Bragg* that night that placed him, a newly minted lieutenant general, under the command of his senior in rank but fellow lieutenant general, *Polk*, as wing commander. Some historians have thus suspected that *Hill* was in no hurry to report to *Polk* and may not have tried his utmost to find him.

Further Reading

Connelly, *Autumn of Glory*, 208–15; Bridges, *Lee's Maverick General*; 208–12; Parks, *General Leonidas Polk*, 333–37; Cozzens, *This Terrible Sound*, 294–98.

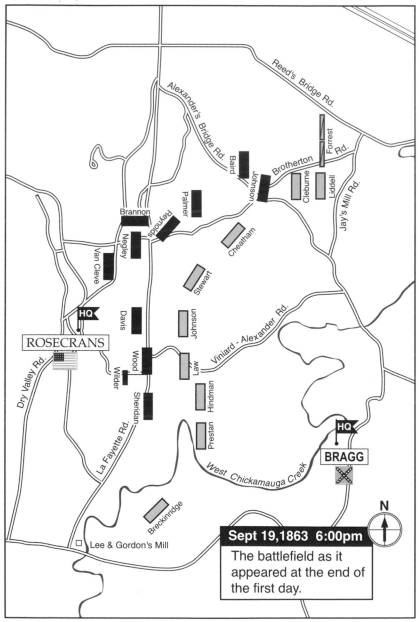

Sept 19,1863 6:00pm

The battlefield as it
appeared at the end of
the first day.

Overview of the Second Day, September 20, 1863

Polk's failure to see that his subordinate *Hill* received and understood his orders resulted in *Bragg's* "day-dawn" attack going in three hours late, after the Union left had built log breastworks and been further reinforced by Rosecrans. The lead Confederate division, John C. *Breckinridge's*, succeeded in getting around the Union left flank, but reinforcements were not in place to support this success—another result of *Polk's* lack of preparation—and it was driven back. The other divisions of the Confederate right launched courageous but piecemeal and uncoordinated attacks against the front of Thomas's by now well-protected lines and were slaughtered.

Shortly before midday *Longstreet* advanced his wing, properly ranged in depth to exploit a breakthrough, and happened to strike a portion of the Union line recently vacated by Wood's division as a result of a mix-up in orders from Rosecrans. *Longstreet's* powerful attacking column roared through the gap. Despite valiant efforts by several Federal units, particularly a number of artillery batteries and the infantry of Sheridan's division, their onslaught proved for a time unstoppable, and the entire Union center and right collapsed in a rout that carried them—along with McCook, Crittenden, and Rosecrans himself—all the way back to Chattanooga.

On the Union left, however, Thomas's by now heavily reinforced XIV Corps continued to stand, and some of the remnants of the broken Union center rallied on a chain of hills on the right rear of Thomas's position. Thomas went there and as senior officer took command on the field, coordinating the defense and infusing new confidence into the troops. With the aid of timely reinforcement by Maj. Gen. Gordon Granger, who marched from Rossville on his own responsibility with a division of his Reserve Corps, Thomas held on to his position throughout the afternoon, despite repeated furious assaults by *Longstreet's* wing trying to complete its success. Receiving orders to withdraw from Rosecrans, who by now was in Chattanooga, Thomas pulled out about dark, ending the battle.

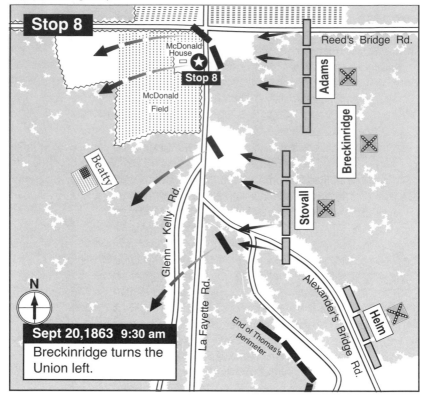

STOP 8 McDonald House   9:30 A.M.

Breckinridge Flanks the Union Line

Directions *Turn around and drive back* in the direction from which you came on ALEXANDER'S BRIDGE ROAD. *Proceed* 2.8 miles (past four different intersections) to LA FAYETTE ROAD. *Turn right.* *Proceed* a little more than 0.2 mile to the Visitor Center parking lot. Park and walk to the front porch of the Visitor Center. Face northeast, toward the traffic light at the intersection of La Fayette Road and Reed's Bridge Road.

Orientation In 1863 the McDonald House stood about where the Visitor Center now stands. The intersection of La Fayette and Reed's Bridge Roads was located in 1863 where it is today.

What Happened Thomas, still commanding the Federal left, wanted to hold the intersection here if he could, though the concentrated semicircle of lines that his 5 divisions had formed during the night stopped about half a mile to your right, about 200 yards west of La Fayette Road. He asked Rosecrans to release James S. Negley's division from service further right.

Rosecrans agreed, but it took time to withdraw Negley from the line and move his brigades north. John Beatty's brigade, first to arrive, was advanced toward this point. The brigade was not large enough to cover the ground assigned to it. Two regiments were deployed here, straddling the road diagonally, facing northeast, as you are. The other two regiments were deployed further south, facing east, in a vain effort to maintain contact with Thomas's left flank.

At 9:30 A.M. the Confederate attack that *Bragg* had ordered for a much earlier hour finally began, with the division of former U.S. vice president John C. *Breckinridge* advancing on the Confederate right. His line moved due west, straight toward you, with its right (northern) flank on Reed's Bridge Road. Two and a half of *Breckinridge's* three brigades passed around Thomas's solid battle lines all but untouched. They struck Beatty's thin-stretched brigade, and it went to pieces. The troops occupying the ground where you now stand put up a brief fight, but they were outnumbered, flanked, and soon found themselves cut off from the rest of the army by the rampaging Confederates. They had to retreat directly westward (behind you and to your right) into the foothills and spurs of Missionary Ridge, where they spent the rest of the day endeavoring to rejoin their brigade. The other fragment of Beatty's brigade fled southward (to your right) into Kelly Field.

Breckinridge, realizing he was beyond the Federal left flank, turned his division south, placing one brigade on each side of the La Fayette Road. The third brigade had brushed against the northern edge of Thomas's lines around Kelly Field (see stop 10) and had become fragmented. With two brigades, however, *Breckinridge* was in position to do serious mischief to the Union army, possibly even wrecking Thomas's forces around Kelly Field and cutting off the Union retreat to Chattanooga. At 10:30 A.M., *Breckinridge* gave the order to advance, and his line swept southward, parallel to La Fayette Road.

Analysis

"The movement seemed exceedingly unwise," Beatty later wrote regarding Thomas's order to place the brigade in this position. He protested the order at the time, but to no avail. Events proved him right. Thomas had made one of his rare mistakes by ordering Beatty this far up La Fayette Road. He would have been better advised to have ignored Reed's Bridge Road until he had enough troops to hold its intersection with La Fayette Road and to have covered his left with the reserves he already had available in Kelly Field rather than waiting for Negley's division coming up from the south. Beatty's brigade simply could not cover that much ground.

A portrait of General Braxton Bragg. After a wartime photograph. BLCW 3:601

Facing page: *On the Confederate Line of Battle "with Fate against Them"* (detail). From a painting by Gilbert Gaul. BLCW 4:frontis

Bragg had finally succeeded in his original purpose of getting beyond the northern flank of the Union army. The question now was whether this success would be supported – and how. Another three or four Confederate brigades in this position, ready to come in directly behind *Breckinridge*, would have been disastrous for the Federals. *Bragg* had made the troops available to *Polk*, but that general – by neglecting to prepare for the attack – had failed to get them into position. *Bragg* had also opted, in his revised battle plans made the night before, for an additional system of supporting the original attack, one very popular with Civil War generals: the oblique attack. As soon as *Breckinridge* became engaged, the next Confederate division would attack and then the next and so on down the line to the south. Thus *Breckinridge* could be supported not only by troops coming up behind him but by the troops next on his left assaulting the front of the Federals he was currently hitting in flank and rear. If it worked, it would roll the whole Union army up into a disorganized and broken mob, cut off from retreat to Chattanooga. By the time the action swept on from this point about midmorning, the first step of *Bragg's* plan, at least, had worked very well indeed.

Further Reading   Cozzens, *This Terrible Sound*, 323 – 26; Tucker, *Chickamauga*, 233 – 36; Woodworth, *A Deep Steady Thunder*, 67 – 69.

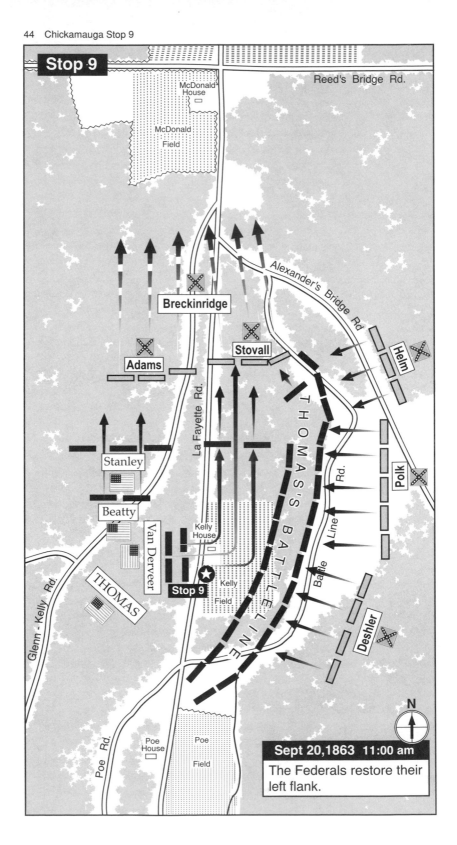

Stop 9

McDonald House

Reed's Bridge Rd.

McDonald Field

Alexander's Bridge Rd.

Breckinridge

Stovall

Adams

Helm

La Fayette Rd.

Stanley

Polk

T H O M A S ' S   B A T T L E   L I N E

Beatty

Van Derveer

Kelly House

THOMAS

Stop 9

Kelly Field

Battle Line Rd.

Deshler

Glenn - Kelly Rd.

Poe Rd.

Poe House

Poe Field

N

Sept 20,1863   11:00 am

The Federals restore their left flank.

STOP 9

Kelly Field   11:00 A.M.

Van Derveer Saves the Union Left

Directions

Turn right from the Visitor Center parking lot. *Proceed* 0.8 mile to the Kelly House on your left. *Turn left* into the parking area in front of the house. Walk back in the direction from which you came to about the end of the rail fence. Face north, back toward the Visitor Center.

Orientation

La Fayette Road is on your left. To your right and in front of you is Kelly Field. Behind you is the reconstructed Kelly farmhouse. Thomas's main battle line was located just beyond the tree line to your right.

What Happened

Breckinridge's two brigades advanced southward down La Fayette Road from the neighborhood of the Visitor Center toward where you now stand. In the woods to the left of the road (to your left front), Brig. Gen. Dan *Adams's* Brigade clashed with the Union brigade of Col. Timothy R. Stanley. Stanley, aided by the rallied remnants of Beatty's brigade, prevailed and drove *Adams's* brigade back, minus its commander, who was left wounded on the field to become a prisoner.

On this side of the road, however, directly in front of you, Brig. Gen. Marcellus A. *Stovall's* regiments, while not penetrating as far south, posed an even greater threat, with the potential to roll up Thomas's entire line, then hotly engaged to its front (see stops 10, 11, 12). The Federals had plenty of troops around Kelly Field, but the Confederates had momentum.

Stovall struck the westernmost extension of Thomas's lines, scattering the defenders almost immediately and pushing on. About 300 yards to your right, a brigade of Palmer's division pulled out of its reserve position and swung north to face the onrushing Confederates, only to come apart under the devastating fire from the woods.

Coming up from a reserve position farther south with orders merely to support Thomas's line, Van Derveer's brigade marched out of the woods on your left. Van Derveer's two lines of battle, each of two regiments, were deployed parallel to La Fayette Road, their right flank about even with you, their left extending to within 200 yards of the fast-shooting Rebels on the north edge of the field. Around them was pandemonium. Through a haze of white powder smoke, blue-clad figures dashed about the field in disorder, past the blazing buildings of the Kelly Farm. The crash of artillery and rifle fire came not only from the north but also from east and south (your right and rear), where the whole semicircle of Thomas's lines was under attack from the front.

Van Derveer determined that the greatest threat lay to the north (in front of you) and wheeled his brigade across the field in front of you, each line pivoting on its left while the right swung forward and to your right across the open field until the whole brigade, still deployed in two lines, faced north. *Stovall's* men were just emerging into the open field, and the fire of Van Derveer's first line halted them and pushed them back into the fringe of trees. Then Van Derveer's second line advanced through the first and charged. Other Northern regiments joined them, and the whole Union force in Kelly Field surged forward. *Stovall* had no more chance than Beatty had had two hours before. His troops fled northward, and some of the Federals pursued to the edge of McDonald Field before withdrawing into Thomas's perimeter.

Analysis

As much as any incident in the war, this encounter was a factor of the fighting qualities of a superior combat unit. The soldiers of Van Derveer's brigade were veterans of long service under good officers. Their regiments boasted some of the most enviable combat records of the army and had served long together. They trusted each other and their officers.

Upon first contact with the enemy in Kelly Field, Van Derveer's men had nearly every possible disadvantage. They were taken by surprise from an unexpected direction at a time when they believed themselves behind their own lines. They were flanked at close range, caught in the open by troops concealed in woods, and the troops around them were in panic and disorder. Nevertheless, they remained cool, executed a difficult maneuver under fire, and attacked boldly. That was all that was needed to allow the Union superiority in numbers to take effect.

That superiority in numbers was another factor in the Federal success here. Thomas had ample reserves arrayed behind this compact semicircle of lines to meet almost any emergency—provided they could resist panic in the shock of sudden setbacks such as the appearance of *Stovall* in Kelly Field. Some of these troops (Van Derveer's, for example) would not have been available there two hours earlier, a fact that emphasizes the significance of *Polk's* failure to attack at dawn as ordered by *Bragg*.

Finally, *Adams* and *Stovall* fought alone. The troops that *Bragg* had hoped would be aiding their efforts were waiting idly in reserve or hammering vainly at the front of Thomas's lines. The struggle there will be discussed at the next three stops.

The 9th Ohio Regiment, the right regiment in Van Derveer's second line (entering the field in a line that paralleled the road, its right flank passed about where you now stand as it began to pivot around to face as you do), was composed of German Americans from Cincinnati. It marched and fought to German-language commands, and it had a reputation for impetuous bayonet charges such as the one that had re-captured a battery during the first day's fighting here at Chickamauga (optional excursion 4). Deployed in front of the 9th were their good friends of the 2nd Minnesota, another of the army's premier regiments. As the Minnesotans drove *Stovall's* men back into the woods, Capt. Jeremiah Donahower, Company E, 2nd Minnesota, heard Col. August Kammerling of the 9th shouting something in unintelligible German. Then the men of the 9th passed through the Minnesotans' line, leveled their bayonets, and charged—without orders from a higher authority. While Donahower gaped, his first sergeant ran out in front of the company shouting, "Don't let the Ninth Ohio charge alone!" He was followed by every member of Company E. At this point Col. James George of the 2nd rode up to ask Donahower just what his company was doing without orders, but all Donahower could do was shrug and run after them. George may have shrugged too. At any rate, he ordered the rest of the regiment forward, joining the charge that cleared the Union flank of live Rebels.

Further Reading

Cozzens, *This Terrible Sound*, 326–37; Tucker, *Chickamauga*, 234–43; Woodworth, *A Deep Steady Thunder*, 70–73.

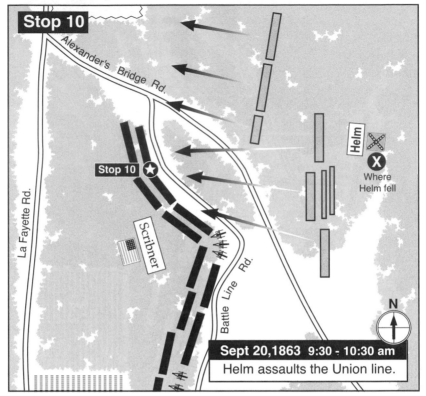

STOP 10   Thomas's Battle Line   9:30–10:30 A.M.

Helm Assaults the Union Line

Directions   *Proceed* north 0.5 mile to ALEXANDER'S BRIDGE ROAD. *Turn right.*
                        Proceed 0.3 mile to BATTLE LINE ROAD. *Turn right* and park in the
                        parking area on the right. Walk a few feet farther to the 10th
                        Wisconsin Monument (the soldier holding the flag).

Orientation   Face east, toward Battle Line Road (the road nearest to you).
                        Behind you are the woods and, beyond them, Kelly Field. In
                        front of you is first Battle Line Road and, beyond a triangle
                        of open woods, Alexander's Bridge Road. At the time of the
                        battle, this area was a glade or open area extending forward
                        about 200 yards in front of you. Today, thick woods begin just
                        120 yards in front of you and to your left. Of course, Battle
                        Line Road did not exist at the time of the battle but was
                        built later to follow the line held by Thomas on this day. You
                        are standing at an angle in the Union line, where Brig. Gen.
                        John H. King's brigade of regular U.S. Army troops (to your
                        left rear) connected with Scribner's brigade (extending to
                        your right, along Battle Line Road). Scribner's men faced in

the direction you are facing. The Confederates came into view on the other side of the glade about 200 yards away.

What Happened

When *Breckinridge* launched his attack at 9:30 A.M., Brig. Gen. Ben Hardin *Helm's* brigade advanced against this portion of the line. After the Confederates appeared within easy rifle shot at the other side of the glade, Northern troops waited silently as *Helm* and his officers carefully dressed their ranks with as close to parade-ground precision as the terrain permitted. The Federal officers hoped to shock and surprise the Confederates with a sudden volley at close range, thus demoralizing them and driving them back. In part, the tactic was successful, for the Confederates were apparently unable to discern the angle of the Union line where you now stand. They thought the Union line continued to your left as it did to your right. The center of *Helm's* brigade advanced directly toward you, and his line extended about 200 yards to either side. When the Union line opened fire, the half of *Helm's* brigade to your right was driven back, but the half on your left broke loose from the brigade and advanced across the front of King's brigade, drawing fire but taking only moderate casualties. It eventually wound up aiding in the destruction of John Beatty's brigade (see stop 8).

Helm was with the half of his brigade that had been repulsed and twice rallied his men to renew the assault. Each time they were the targets of Federal artillery posted 350 yards to your right (see stop 11) and of every Federal rifle between here and there—more than a full brigade—as well as some of King's troops. The result was predictable and bloody. The brigade was subsequently withdrawn several hundred yards to the east (in front of you) to rest and regroup.

Analysis

Helm's brigade was wasted in these futile assaults partly because the Union line here was strongly manned and, by this time, protected by log-and-rail barricades, and partly because of *Polk's* lack of preparation. This lack affected them in three ways: (1) They had no information on the exact location of the Union line and thus broke apart rather than converging on the angle (here). (2) They attacked alone and unsupported. *Cleburne* was to join the attack on their left (your right) but was delayed because *Polk* had not advised him to have his brigades properly aligned and prepared for the attack. Thus the Federals could concentrate a devastating fire on *Helm's* lonely half-brigade. (3) They made the third attack (in which *Helm* fell) in a vain attempt to support their comrades of *Adams's* and *Stovall's* brigades, who were fighting unsupported on the fringes of Kelly Field (see stop 9). Because of

Polk's poor preparation, no reserves were positioned to come up behind *Adams* and *Stovall* in a timely fashion and make their need for support from *Helm* less desperate. As it was, *Helm's* men had to renew an all but suicidal attack because it was the only option available.

Vignette

Brig. Gen. Ben Hardin *Helm* was a 32-year-old Kentucky lawyer, a graduate of West Point (class of 1851), and the husband of Emily Todd. That last point was more significant than the other two, for Emily's half-sister Mary was the wife of Abraham Lincoln. *Helm* had declined a commission from his brother-in-law at the beginning of the war, choosing to go south instead. Now he commanded the "Orphan Brigade" in the Army of Tennessee. When the order came for the advance that morning, *Helm* was sitting under a tree, talking with one of his colonels. Receiving the order, *Helm*, as one of his men wrote in his diary that night, "got up and mounted his horse, laughing and talking as though he was going on parade." In the last futile charge of the Orphan Brigade that morning, *Helm* galloped toward the Federal breastworks but fell from his horse mortally wounded. The place where he fell is about 280 yards directly in front of you. A pyramid of cannonballs now marks the spot and can be reached by walking down the trail that you see leading into the woods on the far side of the clearing.

Further Reading

Cozzens, *This Terrible Sound*, 319–28.

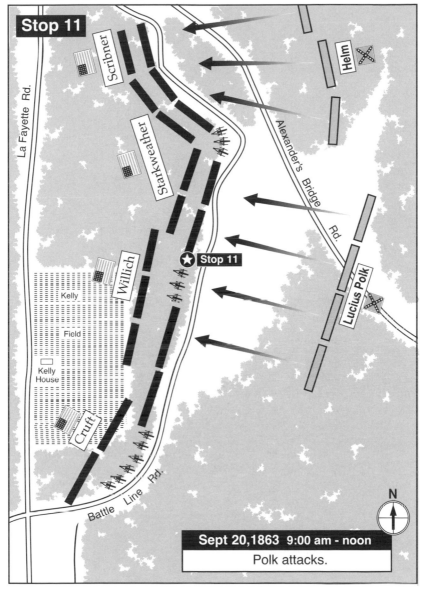

STOP 11   Thomas's Battle Line   9:00 A.M.–noon

Breaking the Confederate Assaults

Directions   *Proceed straight ahead* 0.2 mile to the guns and monument of the 4th Indiana Battery (these will be the next cannon you come to). Just past the cannon, park in the turnout on the right. Face east, the direction the cannons are pointing.

Orientation   This is the easternmost point of Thomas's curving line around Kelly Field. On your left and right the line curves back slightly toward La Fayette Road. The Confederates advanced through the woods directly in front of you, endeavoring to drive the Federals away from log breastworks at your present position and along the line to your right and left. The position where you now stand was a salient, a protruding angle, of Thomas's line. Federals here could to some degree enfilade, or fire into the flanks of, Confederates attacking the Union line for a considerable distance on either side. This is almost undoubtedly why the guns of the 4th Indiana Battery were placed here.

What Happened   *Polk* followed *Breckinridge's* assault with a further series of disjointed, piecemeal attacks on this strongly held Union position. All the attacks were bloody failures. The guns of the 4th Indiana Battery helped repulse *Helm's* attacks to your left (see stop 10).

   Polk, at 10:00 A.M., ordered Maj. Gen. Patrick R. *Cleburne* to advance his division. Though he was one of the best division commanders of the war, *Cleburne* had had no previous warning that he was slated for a morning assault. Consequently, his division was poorly deployed and went into action in a halting and stumbling manner. As they advanced, his brigades ran afoul of each other and of *Stewart's* neighboring division. Each of them ended up fighting its own battle, alone, unsupported, and badly enfiladed. It was not one of *Cleburne's* better days in the war. The result was predictable. *Cleburne's* troops charged with their accustomed élan, but their valor was wasted. One of his brigades reached to within about 50 yards of the Union lines in front of where you now stand and extending about 200 yards to your right. The other two brigades came to grief still farther down the line in that direction.

   Polk was not finished yet, launching the divisions of *Liddell* and Brig. Gen. States Rights *Gist* (yes, that really was his name) behind that of *Breckinridge*. They struck the line to your left. The brigade of Col. Peyton H. *Colquitt*, advancing over the same ground, repeated the experience of *Helm's* brigade, even to the detail of *Colquitt's* own death in battle. In each case, troops from this position, including the 4th Indiana Battery, whose guns you see here, raked the lines of the attacking Confederates with a deadly enfilade fire. Farther to the left, some of *Liddell's* and *Gist's* men scored limited successes over the Union defenders, but these small breakthroughs were quickly smothered by Thomas's alert use of his ample reserves.

Analysis

The key factors in this sector were (1) a skillful Union defense and (2) a blundering Confederate attack.

Thomas and his subordinates had selected a strong, compact position and improved it with makeshift fieldworks constructed early that morning out of logs and fence rails. Manned by veteran troops led by experienced officers, this position would have presented a daunting problem for any attacking column.

As it was, *Polk's* mismanagement aggravated the situation, and his delay ensured failure. Sunrise had found Thomas with substantial but not quite so numerous reserves. Even more important, it found most of his troops with as yet no breastworks. Maj. Gen. John M. Palmer, whose lines began about 300 yards to your right, stated after the war that had *Polk* attacked the unprepared Federals at daybreak, "the battle would not have lasted an hour," because his own troops would have been routed and "gone to Chattanooga on the run." Whether or not he was right, a timely attack would unquestionably have inflicted far higher Federal casualties and had a much better chance of success.

Finally, *Polk's* lack of preparation and late notice to his subordinates led to an attack that was piecemeal and uncoordinated, squandering what little chance remained that the men of his wing of the army could achieve success through all their incredible sacrifices.

Further Reading

Cozzens, *This Terrible Sound*, 338–56; Tucker, *Chickamauga*, 233–50; Woodworth, *A Deep Steady Thunder*, 59–73.

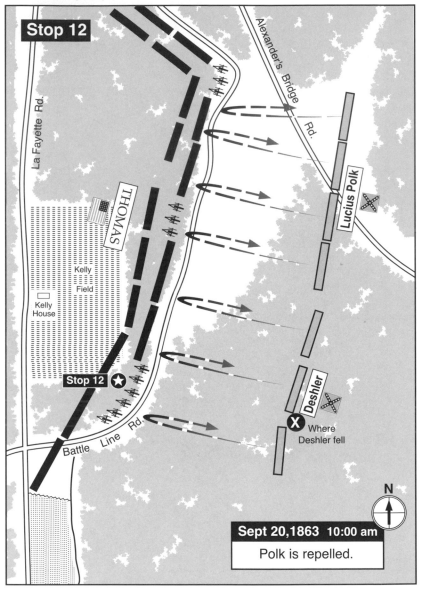

Stop 12

Alexander's Bridge

La Fayette Rd.

Rd.

THOMAS

Lucius Polk

Kelly
Field

Kelly
House

Stop 12 ★

Deshler

X Where
Deshler fell

Battle Line Rd.

N

Sept 20,1863 10:00 am

Polk is repelled.

STOP 12   Thomas's Battle Line   10:00 A.M.

Repulse of *Deshler's* Brigade

Directions   *Proceed straight ahead* 0.3 mile to the sign pointing to the King
                     Monument and the guns and monument of Battery F, 1st
                     Ohio Artillery. Park in the turnout on the right. Note that
                     Col. Edward King, whom the monument commemorates, fell
                     in the late afternoon's fighting. That action will be discussed

when you return here for stop 20. Face east, the direction the cannons are pointing.

Orientation

You are standing near Thomas's breastworks facing the direction his soldiers did. Brig. Gen. James *Deshler's* Confederates advanced directly toward you. Behind you is a gap in the woods, allowing you a glimpse of Kelly Field and Kelly House.

What Happened

Along this section of line, as at the previous two stops, Union troops held firm throughout *Polk's* morning assaults. This position gives you an appreciation of the relationship of Thomas's battle line to Kelly Field. *Deshler's* attack toward your front was simultaneous with the fight between *Stovall* and Van Derveer (and others) in Kelly Field behind you (stop 9). This position also gives you the opportunity to view the ground over which *Deshler's* brigade (of *Cleburne's* division) made its unsuccessful attack and the position from which the Federals of Hazen's brigade, covered by log breastworks, easily repulsed them. *Deshler* himself was killed on a knoll about 180 yards in front of you and somewhat to your right.

Directly to your right, beyond the woods, *Stewart's* division of *Longstreet's* wing attacked in the area of Poe Field, with similar results. By noon the Confederates on this front had fought themselves out, and a four-hour lull ensued in this sector.

Analysis

The breastworks are gone now, but they were the deciding factor. Without them, Hazen's men might (or might not) have held this ground, but their casualties would have been much higher. That it was so easy for them was an object lesson in the value of fieldworks and an indication of why by this point in the war soldiers and their officers were beginning to use them with increasing frequency.

Vignette

Brig. Gen. William B. Hazen wrote in his report of the battle that the Confederates assaulted "with a fury never witnessed upon the field either of Shiloh or Stone's River. The repulse was equally terrific and final. . . . The value of this simple breastwork will be understood since my loss behind it this day was only about 13 men during a period of more stubborn fighting than at Shiloh or Stone's River, when the same brigade at each place lost over 400 men."

Further Reading

Cozzens, *This Terrible Sound*, 338–56; Tucker, *Chickamauga*, 233–50; Woodworth, *A Deep Steady Thunder*, 59–73.

Further Exploration   A yellow-blazed trail leads from just the other side of Battle Line Road eastward to the place (marked by the usual pyramid of cannonballs) where *Deshler* fell, allowing you to view the ground over which his brigade attacked.

Headquarters in the Field. BLCW 1:398

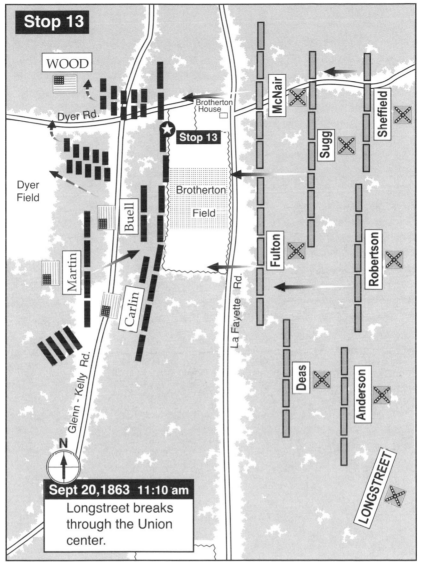

STOP 13   Brotherton Field   11:10 A.M.

Breakthrough

Directions   *Proceed* about 0.3 mile to LA FAYETTE ROAD. *Turn left. Proceed* about another 0.3 mile to DYER ROAD. *Turn right. Proceed* 0.1 mile and park in the turnout on your right, near the edge of the woods. Cross the road and walk along the tree line about 60 yards or until you are about even with the pointed-topped monument up on the ridge to your left. Turn and face that monument, with your back to the woods.

Orientation

To your left is Dyer Road; behind you, the Brotherton Woods. The Brotherton House is in front of you and somewhat to your left. The cannon near it, facing toward you, represent *Bledsoe's* Missouri Battery, which advanced with the Confederate troops who attacked here. The monuments along the ridge in front of you commemorate units that fought there the previous afternoon. The place where you are standing was near the middle of the line of Wood's division during the morning. A rail fence ran along the edge of the woods, and Wood's men had used the rails and a few logs to construct low breastworks.

What Happened

About 11:00 A.M. Wood received a garbled written order from Rosecrans, who had established his headquarters on a knoll about half a mile west of here, out of sight beyond Brotherton Woods (at the edge of which you're standing) and Dyer Field. Based on the incorrect assumption that Brannan's division, next on Wood's left, had pulled out and moved to support Thomas, Rosecrans directed Wood to "close up" on the division of Reynolds and "support" it. Because Brannan's division was between Wood's and Reynolds's, the order made no sense. To "close up" on Reynolds would have indicated a sideways movement–what Rosecrans intended–but to "support" Reynolds, with Brannan still in between, would require dropping out of line and marching around Brannan. Wood did the only thing he could think of to obey the order, pulling his division back out of line and marching it north to come up behind Reynolds. This left a yawning 600-yard gap in the Federal line at the worst of all possible times and places.

Longstreet was about to launch his main blow, and it was aimed straight at Brotherton Field. Like *Polk* on the left, *Longstreet* had three divisions stacked one behind the other here; unlike *Polk*, *Longstreet* was able to advance the divisions in support of each other. The lead division struck this line shortly before 11:30, and by that time only a single, understrength Federal brigade had been able to move into the gap left by Wood's departure. It took position along the tree line just to your right but was almost immediately overrun. The other brigade of Davis's division, farther to your right, beyond Brotherton Field, was also routed, as was the trailing brigade of Wood's division, caught in march column on Glenn-Kelly Road (behind you on the other side of the woods) as it prepared to follow the rest of the division north. The victorious Rebels swept on through the woods to the north and west.

Analysis

Wood's whole division would have had its hands full holding this position against the massive attacking column *Longstreet* launched against it. The single brigade that tried to hold this line after Wood's departure never had a chance. Its line was overrun directly from the front almost before the Confederates swept around both its flanks, which they did at once since there was no one to stop them.

The key to the Federal disaster here, of course, was Wood's withdrawal. Rosecrans was at the best of times nervous and high-strung. During the hectic days of campaigning leading up to the battle, he had denied himself food and sleep. In this state he made the mistake of issuing the order to Wood without sufficient effort to verify the supposed facts on which it was based.

Even at that, Rosecrans might have avoided disaster when his subordinate generals caught his obvious mistake. Ordinarily, such an order simply would not have been carried out. This one was, however, as a result of another of Rosecrans's unpleasant habits. He had taken to publicly and unprofessionally browbeating officers whose performances displeased him. Wood, who was an excellent officer, had in the last few days twice been the victim of such outbursts, each time for alleged failure to obey orders instantly and unquestioningly. He was apparently anxious to avoid further rebuke.

Further Reading   Cozzens, *This Terrible Sound*, 357–73; Tucker, *Chickamauga*, 250–77; Woodworth, *A Deep Steady Thunder*, 74–83.

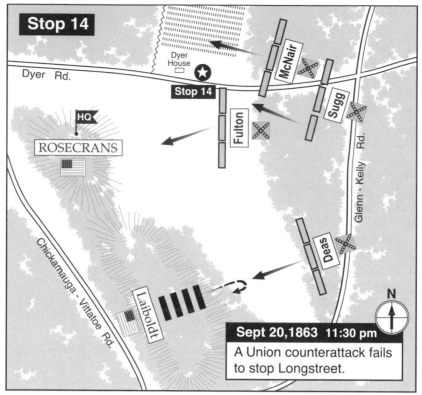

Stop 14

Dyer House

Dyer Rd.

Stop 14

McNair

Sugg

Fulton

Glenn - Kelly Rd.

HQ

ROSECRANS

Deas

Chickamauga - Vittatoe Rd.

Laiboldt

N

Sept 20,1863 11:30 pm

A Union counterattack fails to stop Longstreet.

STOP 14   Dyer Field   11:30 A.M.

Expanding the Breakthrough

Directions

Proceed straight ahead a little over 0.4 mile, just beyond the site of the Park Service tablet for the field hospital of Baird's division of the XIV Corps. Park in the turnout on the right. Walk back along the road about 50 yards, then turn around and face west (the direction you were just driving) along Dyer Road.

Orientation

A wooded hill rises on your left about 500 yards away. Between the hill and Glenn-Kelly Road was a tanyard (where hides were worked into finished leather). It was a clutter of shacks, ash hoppers, tanning pits, and niter vats. The buildings of Dyer Farm were located directly in front of you. The large open area all around you is Dyer Field, and at the time of the battle it was covered with stubble. Across the place where you now stand moved *Johnson's* division as it continued its penetration after its breakthrough in Brotherton Field.

What Happened

At noon, September 20, 1863, the peaceful panorama now spread before you was a scene of incredible pandemonium.

As the front-line troops of *Johnson's* division stood where you now do, they saw in the field to their right front the disorganized fugitive remnants of the divisions of Wood and Van Cleve fleeing northward and westward, while officers struggled to rally some of them in support of a line of reserve artillery on the ridge at the far edge of the field to your right front (now marked by monuments and cannon). Other blue-coated troops, as well as canvas-topped supply wagons, fled in confusion down the road straight ahead to the west. On the open spur of the hill south of the road, 400 yards to your left front, Rosecrans himself, along with his headquarters personnel, was hurriedly mounting up and preparing to betake himself to safer parts (under the trees on that knoll, in the distance, you may just be able to make out the cannonball pyramid marking the site of Rosecrans's headquarters). Nearby the gunners of a Federal battery frantically rammed home charges and blasted away at more targets than they could hope to hit. On the flank of the hill still further to the left, just above the tanyard, a Union brigade was drawn up in what soldiers of that day called "closed battalion column," that is, the four regiments each arrayed in line of battle, one behind the other, with about ten yards separating each regimental line from the one in front of it and the one behind it—a handy formation in which to move troops around the battlefield. Altogether, the scene was one to make the Rebels' breath come short even if they had not just charged all the way from the other side of La Fayette Road.

The Federal brigade on the forest-topped hillside on your left, above the tanyard, belonged to Maj. Gen. Philip Sheridan's division, which was then in motion along the line as part of Rosecrans's general shuffling of units in the army's continued slide to the north. As Confederate troops swept into the tanyard and Dyer Field, the brigade launched a desperate bayonet charge in hopes of stemming the Confederate tide and restoring the Union line. It was a forlorn hope. Every minute, more Confederate formations were moving out of the woods along the full length of Dyer Field. As each Federal regiment in turn reached the bottom of the hill it was hit simultaneously in front and on both flanks. Within a matter of minutes, the brigade, less nearly 400 casualties, had become part of the disorganized mass of fleeting Union soldiers.

Elements of *Johnson's* division pressed forward to the right of Dyer Road, over the ridge there, to capture Union supply wagons and artillery pieces attempting to escape by means of Dry Valley Road, which intersects Dyer Road about 0.4 mile ahead of you. The rest of *Johnson's* troops and the other Confederates now pouring through the gaping hole in Rosecrans's lines began to swing northward to exploit the break-through, even as the southernmost division of *Longstreet's* corps, Maj. Gen. Thomas *Hindman's*, moved to finish off the fragments of the Federal right.

Analysis

Neither Rosecrans nor corps commander Alexander McCook had any idea of the magnitude of the disaster they were facing, which only made the situation worse. The Federal brigade on the hillside above the tanyard, on your left, was commanded by Col. Bernard Laiboldt. He and his men liked their position and wanted to stay there because the slope of the hill allowed each regiment to fire over the heads of their comrades in front—an advantage they would lose if they charged down onto the level ground of the tanyard. Nevertheless, McCook insisted that the charge be made, thus masking three-fourths of the brigade's firepower and exposing its flanks. It probably would not have been able to maintain its position on the hillside in any case, faced as it was with such a massive Confederate assault, but sending it down into the tanyard to its destruction spared the Confederates much of the time and casualties they would have taken in the effort to drive it off the hill. In that case, it might still have withdrawn in tolerably good order instead of being routed. Finally, on the hillside it might have been able to cooperate with the next brigade to the south in Sheridan's column, that commanded by Brig. Gen. William H. Lytle. McCook, however, probably reasoned that quick and aggressive action might restore the Union line. If the breakthrough had been less massive, the counterattack might have worked.

Vignette

In his report, Bushrod *Johnson* described the scene as the Confederates burst out into Dyer Field: "Our lines now emerged from the forest into open ground on the border of long, open fields, over which the enemy were retreating. . . . The scene now presented was unspeakably grand. The resolute and impetuous charge, the rush of our heavy columns sweeping out from the shadow and gloom of the forest into the open fields flooded with sunlight, the glitter of arms, the onward dash of artillery and mounted men, the retreat of the foe, the shouts of the hosts of our army, the dust, the smoke, the noise of fire-arms—of whistling balls and grape-shot and of bursting shell—made up a battle scene of unsurpassed grandeur."

Further Reading

Cozzens, *This Terrible Sound*, 368–75; Tucker, *Chickamauga*, 268–78; Woodworth, *A Deep Steady Thunder*, 83–86.

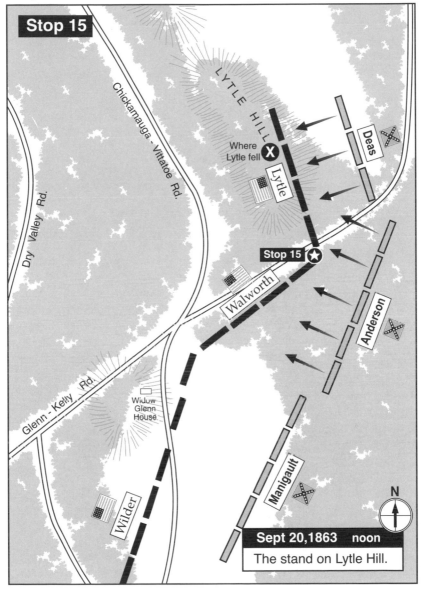

Stop 15

LYTLE HILL

Chickamauga - Vittatoe Rd.

Dry Valley Rd.

Deas

Where
Lytle fell X

Lytle

Stop 15 ⭐

Walworth

Anderson

Glenn - Kelly Rd.

Widow
Glenn
House

Manigault

N

Wilder

Sept 20,1863   noon

The stand on Lytle Hill.

STOP 15   Lytle Hill   noon

Sheridan's Division Makes Its Stand

Directions

Proceed straight ahead 0.3 mile to CHICKAMAUGA-VITTATOE ROAD. *Turn left. Proceed* about 0.5 mile to GLENN-KELLY ROAD. *Turn left* and then immediately *turn right* into the gravel parking lot for the recreation field. Park at the far end of the lot. Walk about 50 yards across the grass toward Glenn-Kelly Road to the sign pointing toward the Lytle Monument. Face east, along Glenn-Kelly Road.

Orientation

Glenn-Kelly Road is on your left. The parking lot and the recreation field are over your right shoulder. Just across Glenn-Kelly Road to your left, a wooded hill rises (this is Lytle Hill). About 30 yards in front of you on the right of the road is the granite monument to the 88th Illinois. Fifty yards ahead of you and even closer to the right-hand side of the road is the monument to the 21st Michigan. About 130 yards ahead of you on the other side of the road, barely visible, are the guns and monument to the 11th Indiana Battery. You are at the right flank of Brig. Gen. William H. Lytle's brigade of Maj. Gen. Philip Sheridan's division, facing the same direction his men did. Angling off over your right shoulder was the line of Col. Nathan Walworth's brigade of Sheridan's division.

What Happened

As Laiboldt's brigade was destroyed in and around the tanyard, Rosecrans ordered Sheridan to bring up his other two brigades in support as rapidly as possible. The two brigades double-quicked over from their position on Widow Glenn Hill, about 500 yards to your right rear, and the first of them, Lytle's brigade, moved up onto the hill on your left. Lytle formed his troops here even as the Confederates, advancing up the other side of the hill, were closing to within 50 yards of his position.

At first Lytle was able to push the Confederates back off the hill, but those in his front, the brigade of Brig. Gen. Zachariah C. *Deas*, got help from the Confederate brigades on either side. Outnumbered and assailed on three sides, Lytle's brigade faced an impossible situation. Lytle himself was enormously popular with his men, and his example of courage did much to steady them. He was hit several times during the brief fight but remained on the field, encouraging his men. As his lines began to give way, another bullet finally brought him down. Without its leader, the brigade streamed to the rear.

Walworth's brigade fared little better, and once Lytle's men gave way, it too had to fall back. The remnant of Sheridan's division then retreated by way of Dry Valley Road and McFarland's Gap, just as the surviving fragments of most of the rest of the army's right and center—including its commander and two of its three corps commanders—were presently endeavoring to get away as best they could.

Analysis

The key factor in *Hindman's* defeat of Sheridan was momentum. *Hindman* had three brigades and was supported by a regiment of *Law's* division on his right (your left), but under ordinary circumstances, Sheridan's two remaining brigades should have been able to stop an assault by a force that size. Sheridan's brigades had had little time to select their position, and though Lytle Hill was a commanding location, both its flanks were exposed. Sheridan's men had no sooner gotten into position than the Confederates were close up to them. The initial success in forcing back the Confederate advance could not compensate for the lost opportunity of carefully selecting a position and of punishing the enemy severely during what would ordinarily have been his lengthy advance toward the defensive position. *Hindman's* men were flushed with their victory over Davis's division and Laiboldt's brigade of Sheridan's and no doubt charged with unusual impetuosity.

Vignette   The sight that met Lytle's men as they first reached the crest and looked down toward the tanyard was another of the shocking panoramas of the battle. Laiboldt's dead and wounded were strewn about seemingly everywhere, while stragglers from various commands ran hither and thither in the confusion. "The sight was truly appalling," recalled Lyman G. Bennett of the 36th Illinois. "The ground was covered with dry grass and old logs which the bursting shells had set on fire. A thick cloud of smoke had risen about as high as our heads and seemed hanging like a funeral pall in the air. Under this we could see, away down the slope of the hill and across the little valley just as far as the eye could reach, moving masses of men hurrying toward us. In our front, not more than seventy or seventy-five yards distant, the enemy's front line lay secreted."

Further Reading   Cozzens, *This Terrible Sound*, 382–89; Tucker, *Chickamauga*, 291–98.

Further Exploration   To see where Lytle's line endeavored to hold the hill (and for a view that is well worth the walk), follow the trail across the road leading up the hill toward the Lytle Monument. This trail more or less follows the brigade's line. The Lytle Monument (a cannonball pyramid from which most of the cannonballs are now missing), a few steps off to the left of the trail, marks the place where Lytle fell. For a view from essentially the same vantage point mentioned in the vignette, follow the trail another 15 yards past the Lytle Monument (i.e., past the 5-yard-long side trail that goes directly to the monument). Then take the side trail to your right and follow it about 30 yards until you come out onto the grassy hilltop. The tanyard was at the bottom of the slope in front of you. Your present position also is that of the rear line of Laiboldt's brigade column before he launched his downhill bayonet charge. By walking forward a few yards you can look northward (to your left) over Dyer Field and see the place where you stood at stop 14. This will give a good perspective on the overall relationship of the action on this end of the field.

General W. H. Lytle, commander of the 1st Brigade of Sheridan's Division. General Lytle was killed in battle on September 20, 1862. BLCW 3:658

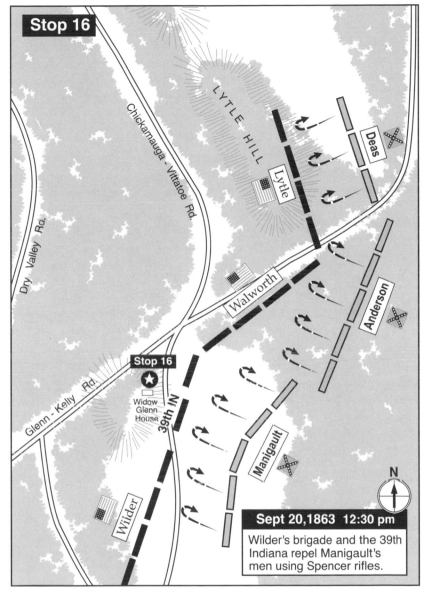

Stop 16

LYTLE HILL

Chickamauga - Vittatoe Rd.

Dry Valley Rd.

Deas

Lytle

Walworth

Anderson

Stop 16

★

Widow Glenn House

39th IN

Manigault

Glenn - Kelly Rd.

Wilder

N

Sept 20, 1863 12:30 pm

Wilder's brigade and the 39th Indiana repel Manigault's men using Spencer rifles.

STOP 16   Widow Glenn Hill   12:30 P.M.

Wilder Strikes Back

Directions   *Leave* the parking lot by the exit furthest from where you stood for stop 15. *Turn left* onto CHICKAMAUGA-VITTATOE ROAD. *Proceed* 0.3 mile (make sure to hold to the right and not take the road that appears to fork to the left – it's one-way going toward you!) to the parking area on your left at the Wilder Tower. Walk to the tower and around to the other side of it.

Face downhill, with your back to Wilder Tower (and the parking lot).

Orientation

You are on Widow Glenn Hill. About 25 yards to your left stood Eliza Glenn's house, Rosecrans's headquarters on September 19. On the twentieth, Wilder's brigade held a position about where you now stand and facing as you do.

What Happened

Advancing on the far left of the Confederate line, Arthur *Manigault's* brigade of *Hindman's* division was completing the destruction of a few remnants of Sheridan's division that were hanging on near this spot. The scene was one of confusion, as the desperate bluecoats strove to resist and the Widow Glenn's house caught fire after being hit by Confederate artillery shells (she and her children had left some time before). Just as Federal resistance appeared to be crumbling, *Manigault's* Confederates got a nasty surprise. As the right flank regiment, in the woods to your left, neared the crest of the ridge, it came face to face—at a range of about 30 yards—with the 39th Indiana Mounted Infantry, coming up the other side. The Hoosiers were dismounted and were equipped with Spencer rifles, and their rapid fire chewed up *Manigault's* right. At the other end of the line, matters were even worse for the Confederates. On the right of the 39th Indiana was Wilder's entire five-regiment brigade of mounted infantry, all armed with the deadly Spencers. They flanked the southern end of *Manigault's* line, sending his brigade reeling backward in retreat all the way to the far side of La Fayette Road.

With *Manigault* disposed of, Wilder examined the situation on his part of the field and decided that his best course was to charge with his entire brigade right through Dyer Field—and through the rear echelons of the Confederate troops deploying there against Federal resistance further north—and make it into Thomas's lines. He believed he not only could get through but also could tear up a good portion of *Bragg's* army in the process. His men were inclined to agree, believing they and their Spencers could go through practically any number of Rebels. It was not to be, however. As Wilder formed up his brigade to move north, he was met by Assistant Secretary of War Charles A. Dana, attached to Rosecrans's headquarters. Dana adamantly forbade Wilder to attack and ordered him to withdraw and to provide Dana with an escort back to Chattanooga. Thus ended the action on this front.

Analysis

Here, as in the fighting around Viniard Field the day before, one of the key factors was the firepower of the Spencer Repeating Rifle. At the same time, this factor was magnified by battlefield conditions – the ridge, the woods, and smoke from gunfire and from the burning Glenn house – that caused the encounter to occur at fairly close range and very much to the surprise of the Confederates, who were already engaged with the right wing of Walworth's brigade just north of here (to your left). Wilder's men, on the other hand, were just coming into the second day's fight and expected from the sound of firing to find Confederates on this side of the ridge. The result, then, was surprised Confederates finding rapid-firing, advancing enemies close in their front and flank.

Wilder could have accomplished a great deal more on this flank if allowed to do so. His men possessed a significant technological advantage as well as plenty of experience and confidence. The brigade also had a position now in the rear of the Confederate troops who were even then swinging north to confront Thomas. The Indiana colonel might just have made good his intention of joining Thomas and seriously disrupting *Longstreet's* wing of the Confederate army.

Vignette

Wilder maintained for years afterward that Dana's order had denied him a major success. Col. Smith D. Atkins, of the 92nd Illinois in Wilder's brigade, agreed wholeheartedly in that assertion. Atkins's analysis of the reason the brigade was held back was simple: "Wilder was daring and desperate; Dana, a coward and an imbecile."

Further Reading

Cozzens, *This Terrible Sound*, 392 – 96; Tucker, *Chickamauga*, 298 – 99.

Union cavalry scouting in front of the Confederate advance. BLCW 3:244

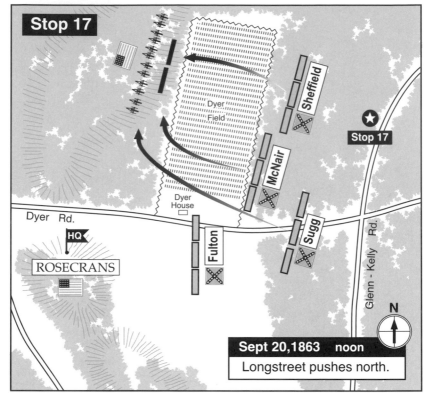

STOP 17   North Dyer Field   noon

Longstreet Pushes North

Directions   *Turn right* from the parking area, returning the way you came. *Proceed* on GLENN-KELLY ROAD past stop 15, beyond the intersection with DYER ROAD, and on for a total of about 0.8 mile. Park in the turnout on the right just beyond the cannonball pyramid for *Longstreet's* headquarters. Walk across the road and stand with your back to the road and facing the ridge on the far side of the open field.

Orientation   You are standing on the eastern edge of Dyer Field. The northern portion of the field is spread out in front of you. The Confederate breakthrough occurred farther south (the direction from which you just came, at your left now) and spread in this direction. Confederate troops moved northward through the field, from your left to your right, and also came out of the woods behind you facing the direction you now do. On the ridge on the far side of the field directly in front (west) of you, several batteries of Union artillery were firing on the Confederates here and farther south in Dyer Field.

What Happened

Some Federal reserve artillery had been positioned on the ridge before the collapse of the Union center, and additional batteries (and some infantry) joined those already there during the midday fighting until, as the divisions of *Johnson* and *Law* moved out across the field, they came under the fire of 29 cannon arrayed on the ridge opposite you. Their presence convinced *Longstreet* to abandon *Bragg's* original plan of swinging south (to drive the Federals into McLemore's Cove) in favor of swinging north, to confront the Union forces still resisting across the field from you.

While *Law's* division attacked straight across the field from your position toward the guns on the ridge, *Johnson's* crossed the southern end of Dyer Field and then turned and advanced along the ridge and on either side of it toward the Federal flank. The assault succeeded as the Union infantry broke for the rear and most of the cannon, their horses killed by the fire of the Confederate infantry, were left as prizes for the Southerners.

Analysis

Longstreet had little choice but to turn north, since he could not afford to leave such powerful forces as were obviously gathering there free to fall on his flanks and rear should he pursue the other Federals toward Chattanooga. Thus by their stubborn resistance, the troops of the Union left and center were already covering the retreat of their comrades on the right.

The line of 29 guns on the ridge opposite you represented a substantial accumulation of artillery in a strong position. Fewer guns had blasted the life out of *Stewart's* temporary breakthrough in Poe Field less then 24 hours earlier. Several factors prevented a repetition. (1) The ridge and tree line on the far (west) side of the field form a position strong against attack from the east (the direction from which you would approach it) but vulnerable to the sort of flank attack that *Johnson* used. (2) Unlike *Bate* the previous afternoon, who had entered Poe Field with most of one brigade, *Hood* eventually launched no less than five brigades against the position across the field. (3) Finally, the guns on the ridge had very little infantry support and such as they did have proved not particularly resolute. Only three regiments of Buell's brigade could be rallied along the rail fence that then ran near the bottom of the hill, and they were badly depleted by casualties suffered this and the previous day and by stragglers lost when the brigade was caught marching northward on Glenn Kelly Road, very near where you now stand, and routed. These infantrymen were demoralized—shock, confusion, fatigue, and the stress of battle had exhausted their supply of courage for that day. When *Hood's* men advanced boldly, these Federals fled, leaving their comrades of the artillery in a hopeless situation. The artillerists had the disciplined drill of loading and firing to hold them to the work and keep their minds off danger, and many of them were going into action for the first time that day. Therefore, they proved considerably less prone to panic.

Further Reading   Cozzens, *This Terrible Sound*, 397–405.

Optional Excursion   If you have time and inclination, an excellent vantage point on the fighting at the north end of Dyer Field, including efforts by Federal infantry to halt or delay the Confederate advance at the extreme northern end of the field, can be gained from the hill on which stands the South Carolina Monument. To reach it, drive on about 0.4 mile to the parking area for the South Carolina Monument on your left. Walk along the path that follows the edge of the woods uphill and then along the gravel road, still going uphill toward the large monument that you see in front of you. The total walk is about 300 yards. Follow the gravel road a few yards as it curves to the left near the crest. Turn to optional excursion 6, South Carolina Monument.

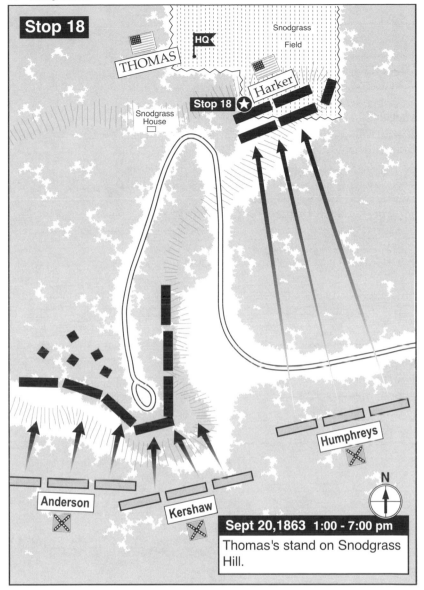

Stop 18

THOMAS

HQ

Snodgrass
Field

Harker

Snodgrass
House

Stop 18 ★

Humphreys

Anderson

Kershaw

N

Sept 20,1863 1:00 - 7:00 pm

Thomas's stand on Snodgrass Hill.

STOP 18   Snodgrass Hill   1:00–7:00 P.M.

The Rock of Chickamauga

Directions   *Proceed straight ahead* about 0.5 mile to VITTATOE ROAD. *Turn left. Proceed* 0.2 mile to a fork in the road. *Take the right fork,* SNODGRASS ROAD, and *proceed* 0.1 mile to Snodgrass House. Park in the turnout on the right, near Snodgrass House. Walk down the open, monument-lined ridge to the monument with a statue of a tiger on top of it. Face to your right, the same way the tiger is looking.

Orientation

Snodgrass House is uphill on your right. In front of you are woods and thickets, but in 1863 the slope in front of you was covered by a woodland so open that visibility was 400 yards. You are now on the line held by Union troops throughout the afternoon, facing as they did. This particular segment was held by Charles G. Harker's brigade of Wood's division. The other troops in this sector were all either refugees from the disaster of the center and right or else reserve elements that Thomas had spared from his Kelly Field position. Thomas's afternoon headquarters was about 300 yards down the slope behind you, marked today by a pyramid of cannonballs.

What Happened

It was for organizing and commanding the stand along this hill and the connecting Horseshoe Ridge (stop 19) that Maj. Gen. George H. Thomas earned the nickname "The Rock of Chickamauga."

Fragments of the units defeated further south had begun to rally on this hill shortly after midday, forming up with fresh, unbloodied units that had been held in reserve there. The bits and pieces of the divisions of Brannan, Negley, and Van Cleve ranged in size from full brigades in tolerably good order to mere remnants of regiments such as the 40 men still with the colors of the 44th Indiana who formed up down the ridge to your left. The area where you now stand was held by troops of Col. Charles G. Harker's brigade, including the 125th Ohio, which had retreated in fairly good order after its fierce battle, delaying the Confederates at the north end of Dyer Field (ahead of you, out of sight beyond the woods about 500 yards).

Thomas had heard the rising roar of firing from Dyer Field, and though his own line was still hotly engaged in front and on his left flank, the rapid approach of the firing on his right and rear prompted him to investigate. Riding toward the vantage point of Snodgrass Hill, he met Wood and accompanied Wood and Harker as the latter's brigade made its stand on the ridge just south of here. When the brigade was forced back, Thomas established his headquarters on the reverse slope of this ridge, then rode along the line to strengthen the men's resolve to stand their ground.

The Confederates who first attacked along this line were South Carolinians of Brig. Gen. Joseph *Kershaw's* brigade, following up their victory in Dyer Field. Theirs was the first of a series of Confederate attacks on this position over a period of six hours that saw some of the fiercest fighting of the war.

Thomas's men remained in position despite the furious assaults until orders arrived from Rosecrans to withdraw from the field.

Analysis

Why did the Federals hold here after being routed further south? There are several reasons:

1. The Confederate attacks were disjointed and uncoordinated. *Hood* had been severely wounded in the fighting in north Dyer Field, and *Longstreet* failed to provide adequate direction for this part of the battle.

2. The Confederate soldiers themselves were exhausted after hours of hard fighting. The Federals were tired as well, but theirs was not the task of charging up these steep hills–again and again–carrying weapons, ammunition, and equipment.

3. Harker's defense was methodical and made use of the terrain. He arranged his brigade in two lines. Between Confederate attacks, one line lay down–sheltered–here at the crest, while the other rested further back the slope behind you. When an attack began, the first line would rise and deliver its fire in a single volley, then fall back and load under the shelter of the hill while the second line moved up to this position to deliver its own volley. The troops were thus exposed only briefly and partially to enemy fire and then only while delivering their own fire. They could reload quickly and efficiently in the standing position yet remain covered by the brow of the hill.

The most important factor in the Union stand was probably Thomas himself and his effect in restoring the confidence and courage of his troops. Historian Peter Cozzens writes: "The presence of Thomas was electrifying. Nearly every soldier in Harker's brigade who left a record of his experiences in the battle mentions having seen Thomas, sitting stolidly amid the noise and confusion, and of the uplifting effect this had on morale."

Vignette

The 125th Ohio was commanded on this day by Col. Emerson Opdycke and earned their nickname "Opdycke's Tigers" (thus the monument). Opdycke had proven himself already one of the finest officers in the army and would eventually become a brigadier general. As the troops here prepared to meet the first Confederate assault shortly after noon, Thomas approached and told Opdycke, "You must hold this position at all hazards." Opdycke replied, "We will hold this ground or go to Heaven from it." They held it until ordered to retire. Of the 314 officers and men who went into battle with the 125th, 105 had become casualties by the end of the day.

Further Reading   Cozzens, *This Terrible Sound*, 417–521.

Note: If you are proceeding on foot as part of the walking tour beginning at optional excursion 6, South Carolina Monument, you may now return to your car by returning to the paved road and walking downhill a little over 500 yards to GLENN-KELLY ROAD. Turn right and walk about one-half mile to your car. *Drive back in the opposite direction of that in which you were just walking* (remember, Glenn-Kelly Road is one-way), past the intersection of VITTATOE ROAD (down which you walked), and stay on GLENN-KELLY ROAD a total of 1.1 miles to LA FAYETTE ROAD. Drive across LA FAYETTE ROAD to ALEXANDER'S BRIDGE ROAD. *Proceed* 0.3 mile (from LA FAYETTE ROAD) to BATTLE LINE ROAD. *Turn right. Proceed* just over 0.5 mile to the sign pointing to the King Monument. Park in the turnout on the right. Face along the road in the direction you were driving. Turn to stop 20.

The Snodgrass Farm-house. The head-quarters of General Thomas on the after-noon of the second day were in the field this side of the house. Horseshoe Ridge lies beyond the house. BLCW 3:666

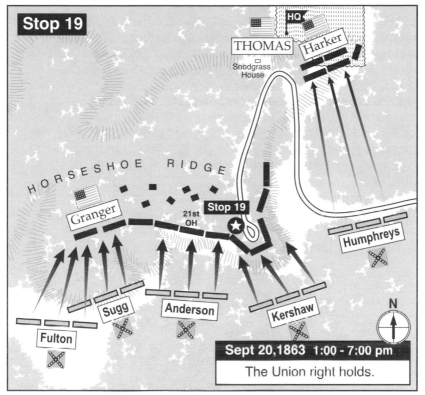

Stop 19

THOMAS | Harker

HQ

Snodgrass House

HORSESHOE RIDGE

Granger

21st OH

Stop 19

Humphreys

Sugg

Anderson

Kershaw

Fulton

N

Sept 20,1863 1:00 - 7:00 pm

The Union right holds.

STOP 19	Horseshoe Ridge 1:00–7:00 P.M.

The Union Right Holds

Directions   *Proceed* in the direction you have been driving about 0.1 mile to a parking area located at the terminus of this road. Walk about thirty yards uphill and to your right to the monument to the 2nd Minnesota (the monument is decorated with a statue of three soldiers with a flag). Face toward the woods nearest the monument (the direction the bronze soldiers are facing).

Orientation   You are standing approximately where the Union line was on the afternoon of September 20, facing the direction the soldiers faced. The Confederates advanced up the hill through the woods toward your position. (The monument here, like several others nearby, is misplaced. The 2nd Minnesota fought further up the ridge.)

What Happened   As the Confederates sought to flank the Union position on Snodgrass Hill (behind you), they moved to take the ridge farther up, here and for several hundred yards to your right.

Thomas extended his meager available forces as far as he could in that direction, and the fighting for this ridgetop was as ferocious as that for the open spur on which Snodgrass House stands. Several times, attacking Confederates of *Kershaw's*, *Hindman's*, and *Johnson's* divisions actually made small lodgments on the ridge, only to be driven off.

While the fighting took place along the ridge all the way from Snodgrass Hill, past where you now stand, and 600 or 700 yards to your right, your present position gives you a feel for the terrain involved.

Vignette

The troops who actually held this point in the line were "scattered detachments of a dozen different commands" gathered up and led into action by Brig. Gen. John Beatty, who had become separated from his own brigade. He later described the action here: "[The] men fought and struggled and clung to that ridge with an obstinate persistence, desperate courage, unsurpassed, I believe, on any field. I robbed the dead of cartridges and distributed them to the men; and once when, after a desperate struggle, our troops were driven from the crest and the enemy's flag waved above it, the men were rallied, and I rode up the hill with them, waving my hat and shouting like a madman. Thus we charged, and the enemy only saved his colors by throwing them down the hill. However much we may say of those who held command, justice compels the acknowledgment that no officer exhibited more courage on that occasion than the humblest private in the ranks."

Further Reading

Cozzens, *This Terrible Sound*, 417–521.

Optional Excursion

A key part of the fighting on Horseshoe Ridge occurred several hundred yards further up the ridge where the 21st Ohio made an epic defensive stand to hold the Union flank until reinforced by the timely arrival of the Army of the Cumberland's Reserve Corps under Maj. Gen. Gordon Granger. If you would like to view the ground where the 21st Ohio made its stand and Granger's troops their timely arrival, walk up the ridge, keeping to the cleared area, which will gradually narrow to the width of a footpath. The path descends a bit to the 21st Ohio Monument, also misplaced. The extreme left flank of the regiment would probably have been a little farther up the path yet, and the regiment's main stand was made at the top of the next rise (still following the path), where you will find a small clearing and various monuments to units of Brig. Gen. James Blair Steedman's division. As you walk to this position, remember that the Confederates were advanc-

ing up the hill from your left, while Steedman's reinforcements came up from your right. Turn to optional excursion 7,
Upper Horseshoe Ridge.

Note: If you are proceeding on foot as part of the walking tour
beginning at optional excursion 6, South Carolina Monument, you should walk downhill (after finishing this stop or
optional excursion 7) toward the parking area. From the parking area, walk down the paved road about 180 yards to the reconstructed log cabin (Snodgrass House) on your left. Leaving
the road, walk on the grass past the cabin and down the monument-lined ridge below it to the monument that has a tiger
on top (125th Ohio Monument). Stand beside the monument,
face to your right (the direction the tiger is looking), and turn
to stop 18.

Brevet Major General Emerson Opdycke. BLCW 4:446

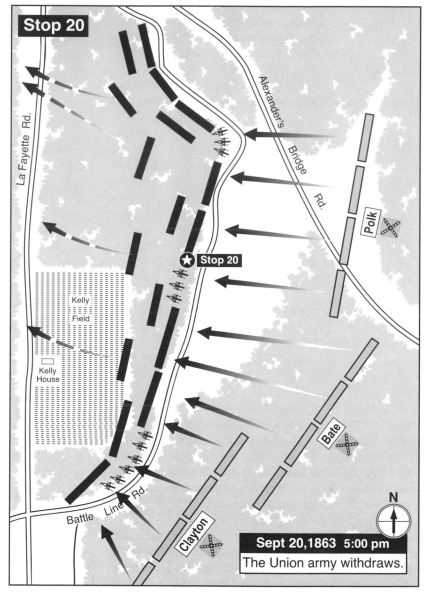

STOP 20   Thomas's Battle Line   5:00 P.M.

Confederate Assault and Union Retreat

Directions   *Drive back* past Snodgrass House a total of about 0.4 mile to
                     GLENN-KELLY ROAD. *Turn left and proceed* 0.6 mile to LA FAYETTE
                     ROAD. Drive across LA FAYETTE ROAD to ALEXANDER'S BRIDGE
                     ROAD. *Proceed* 0.3 mile (from LA FAYETTE ROAD) to BATTLE
                     LINE ROAD. *Turn right. Proceed* just over 0.5 mile to the sign

pointing to the King Monument. Park in the turnout on the right. Face along the road in the direction you were driving.

Orientation

Once again you are on Thomas's battle line, looking along the length of the right side of the breastworks. Again, as during the morning, the Confederates advanced from your left. To your right, a little over 100 yards away, is the monument to Col. Edward King, near the gap that allows you to view Kelly Field beyond.

What Happened

Late in the afternoon, Rosecrans, who was then already back in Chattanooga, issued orders for Thomas to withdraw. At the same time, *Bragg* urged *Polk* to renew the attack by the Confederate right wing to aid the victorious left wing in crushing the Army of the Cumberland. The result was that just as the Confederates launched their new attacks, Thomas's division commanders got orders to pull back. The Confederates, having no knowledge of the withdrawal order, exulted in the apparent success of the attack. A short distance ahead of you, the Eufaula (Alabama) Artillery Battery drove its guns and limbers through the broken-down Union breastworks, unlimbered, and blasted the Federals as they withdrew across Kelly Field. All along the line, in front of you and behind, Confederates surged over the breastworks. Union brigades that had stood all day broke apart during the confused retreat, and the Confederates took many prisoners. Endeavoring to rally troops and direct movements on this part of the field, Colonel King was killed near the cannonball pyramid on your right at about this time. Some Federal brigades got off in fairly good order. As daylight began to fade, *Polk* ordered the attack halted at La Fayette Road.

Analysis

Withdrawing while under attack is one of the most difficult maneuvers to accomplish without going completely to pieces, but the Federals here had no choice but to try. The result was about as good as could have been hoped for under the circumstances. The Union situation was made worse by the fact that Thomas himself was not able to be present in person to direct a coordinated withdrawal from the Kelly Field lines. Instead, he was directing even more crucial operations in trying to salvage the situation into which the rest of the army had fallen. The result here was that each division commander was on his own in getting his troops off the field as best he could, without reference to other units.

For the Confederates, nothing describes this incident as well as the old cliché that nothing succeeds like success. The sight of the Federals finally retiring from the breastworks before which so many Confederates had fallen in vain that day inspired *Polk's* troops to press the attack with redoubled vigor.

Vignette

As darkness settled in and *Polk's* troops swept over Kelly Field, where no Federal offered further resistance, many of the Confederates did not realize that the other wing of the Army of the Cumberland was fighting a separate battle on hills to the west and that even most of this wing had withdrawn more or less intact. Thinking they had completed the destruction of the Union army, the Rebels sent up a cheer so loud that men from both sides remembered it years later. A soldier of the 20th Tennessee wrote, "At sunset . . . everyone seemed wild with joy, from generals down to privates, all joined in the exultant cheer that rang over that blood-stained field. . . . Wild shouts ran from one end of our lines to the other, and even the poor wounded fellows lying about through the woods joined in."

The Federals heard it too, though with very different emotions. Ambrose Bierce described the scene: "Away to our left and rear some of Bragg's people set up 'the rebel yell.' It was taken up successively and passed round to our front, along our right and in behind us again, until it seemed almost to have got to the point whence it started. It was the ugliest sound that any mortal ever heard–even a mortal exhausted and unnerved by two days of hard fighting, without sleep, without rest, without food and without hope. There was, however, a space somewhere at the back of us across which that horrible yell did not prolong itself; and through that we finally retired in profound silence and dejection, unmolested."

Further Reading

Cozzens, *This Terrible Sound*, 488–501.

This concludes the main tour of the Chickamauga battlefield. To return to the Visitor Center, proceed about 0.3 mile to LA FAYETTE ROAD. *Turn right. Proceed about 1.1 mile to the Visitor Center on your left.*

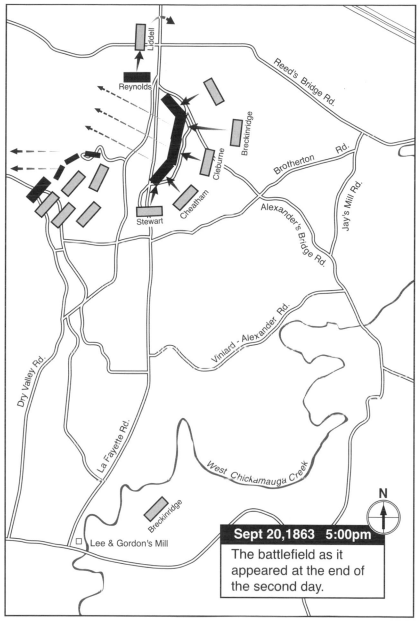

Liddell

Reynolds

Reed's Bridge Rd.

Breckinridge

Cleburne

Brotherton Rd.

Jay's Mill Rd.

Cheatham

Stewart

Alexander's Bridge Rd.

Vinlard - Alexander Rd.

Dry Valley Rd.

La Fayette Rd.

West Chickamauga Creek

Breckinridge

N

☐ Lee & Gordon's Mill

Sept 20,1863   5:00pm

The battlefield as it
appeared at the end of
the second day.

Optional Excursions

The following section contains optional excursions, actually additional stops, that are primarily intended to be visited as part of an enlarged tour, each optional excursion fitting in as noted in the regular stops. Alternatively, you may follow these stops as a sort of secondary tour of some of the less visited and more out-of-the-way sites on the Chickamauga battlefield. To do so, follow the instructions marked "Secondary Tour." Remember that the first optional excursion will take you back in time to a point well before that of the last stop in the main tour (stop 20), in fact, all the way back to the day before the real battle actually started.

To reach the first excursion stop and begin the secondary tour, *turn left* from the Visitor Center and *proceed* 0.1 mile to the traffic light at REED'S BRIDGE ROAD. *Turn right. Proceed* 2.6 miles to REED'S BRIDGE. Park in the turnout on the right, just before the bridge. Turn to optional excursion 1, Reed's Bridge.

A Shell at Headquarters.
BLCW 4:247

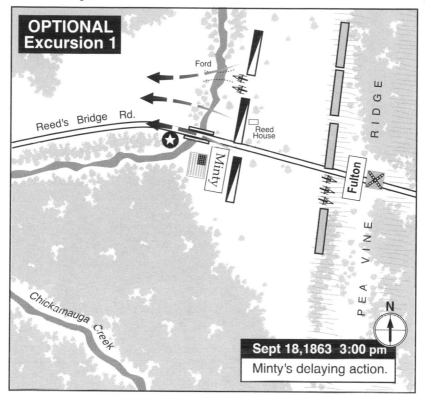

OPTIONAL EXCURSION 1   Reed's Bridge   3:00 P.M., September 18

Johnson Takes the Crossing

Directions   You may remain in your car or get out and stand beside the road. If you do get out, please note that the nearby creek bank is badly undermined and liable to cave in. Therefore, do not climb on it or approach too close to the edge.

Orientation   Face east along the road. The bridge is in front of you. To your left is the road, to your right, Chickamauga Creek, which here makes a bend from flowing northeast to flowing due north. More trees and brush grow along it than did in 1863.

What Happened   The Union cavalry brigade of Col. Robert H. G. Minty had the duty of holding Reed's Bridge as long as possible. Minty deployed his cavalry about a mile farther east. For several hours he fell back skirmishing before the advance of Brig. Gen. Bushrod R. *Johnson's* division, which was tasked with forcing a crossing here. Minty's skillful tactics delayed *Johnson's* approach. Though outnumbered nearly five to one, Minty made particular trouble for *Johnson* as the latter tried to push a column through the gap by which the road traverses Pea Vine Ridge, about 500 yards in front of you (out of sight; the terrain of Pea Vine Ridge has been altered beyond recognition by housing development). Finally, Brig. Gen. John *Gregg's* Tennessee brigade scrambled over the ridge in a line of battle that stretched several hundred yards to the right of the road, flanking Minty. As Minty began his withdrawal to the west bank, Col. John S. *Fulton's* brigade, in column of fours, double-quicked through the gap. One battalion of the 4th U.S. Cavalry, supported by four guns of the Chicago Board of Trade Battery, made a brief stand in the orchard of Reed House, beside the road about 150 yards in front of you (in the patch of open ground you see directly beyond the bridge). The battery then retired to a position about 50 yards to your left and opened fire across the creek to cover the retreat of the battalion of Regulars. The last cavalrymen to cross tried to do what damage they could to the bridge (which Minty described as "a narrow, frail structure . . . planked with loose boards and fence rails"). The 23rd Tennessee, of *Fulton's* brigade, gave a Rebel yell and rushed the bridge. Parting shots from the fleeing cavalrymen felled five of them, including the color-bearer, but the rest stormed across, having driven off the defenders before they could do a thorough job of destruction.

Analysis

A couple of factors aided Minty in his mission of delaying the Confederate advance. *Johnson* had advanced tentatively because he was without a screen of cavalry to warn of enemy forces waiting ahead. He thus feared blundering into a trap with his main force. Pea Vine Ridge proved of particular aid to Minty in that the narrow gap by which the road passed through it channeled *Johnson's* advancing Confederates into a narrow column that made an easy target for Minty's artillery and carbines while denying *Johnson* the use of most of his own firepower as well as his advantage in numbers. Only when *Johnson* pushed troops up and over the ridge in line of battle did he succeed in breaking the impasse.

Chickamauga Creek was a significant military obstacle. An individual might wade or swim across, but organized units (to say nothing of an army's indispensable artillery and supply train) could cross only at the bridges or (with great difficulty) at one of the few fords. The battle of Chickamauga could not have happened as it did if the Confederates had not succeeded in taking these key crossing points. *Johnson's* success here at Reed's Bridge allowed Confederate forces later that afternoon to move upstream (south) to outflank and drive off Col. John T. Wilder's brigade guarding Alexander's

Bridge. By nightfall, Southern troops were in firm possession of both banks of the creek and in position to continue their offensive.

Vignette

Throughout the fight that afternoon, a nagging concern of Minty's was Mrs. Reed, who, with her three children, refused to leave her cabin for a safer location. When entreaty proved useless, Minty gave up and merely warned her to stay inside. As *Johnson's* men poured through the gap in Pea Vine Ridge and the Federals galloped past her cabin in retreat, the woman stood out on her front porch. "You Yanks are running!" she jeered. "Our army is coming! Our friends will not hurt me!" At that moment, a load of canister from the guns of a Confederate battery on the ridge blasted the porch, hurling Mrs. Reed's lifeless body against the front door of her own cabin.

Further Reading

Peter Cozzens, *This Terrible Sound*, 103–14.

TO RETURN TO THE MAIN TOUR

If you would prefer to return to the main tour at this time without viewing Alexander's Bridge, *turn around and drive back* the way you came 1.6 miles to the parking area on your right. Turn to "Overview of the First Day." After reading that section, walk to the nearby cannons and turn to stop 1.

TO CONTINUE WITH THE SECONDARY TOUR

To proceed to optional excursion 2, Alexander's Bridge (the other crossing of Chickamauga Creek seized by the Confederates late on September 18), *turn around and drive back* the way you came 0.6 mile to JAY'S MILL ROAD. *Turn left.* Proceed 1.1 miles to ALEXANDER'S BRIDGE ROAD. *Turn left.* Proceed not quite 0.7 mile to Alexander's Bridge over Chickamauga Creek. Park in the turnout on the right, just before you reach the bridge. Turn to optional excursion 2, Alexander's Bridge.

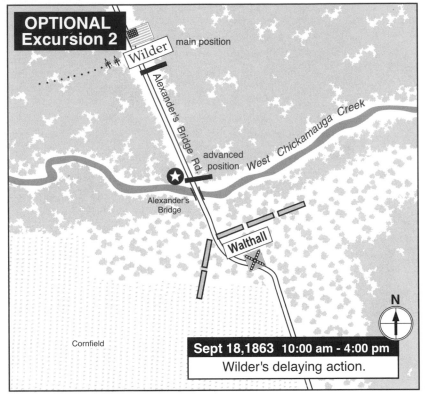

OPTIONAL
Excursion 2

Wilder

main position

Alexander's Bridge Rd.

advanced
position   West Chickamauga Creek

Alexander's
Bridge

Walthall

Cornfield

N

Sept 18, 1863   10:00 am - 4:00 pm
Wilder's delaying action.

OPTIONAL EXCURSION 2

Alexander's Bridge   10:00 A.M.–4:00 P.M., September 18

Wilder Holds On

Orientation

Stand near the road, facing the bridge. The Confederates advanced from the other side of the creek. You are near the position of Wilder's brigade. The terrain here has changed dramatically. The surrounding area was largely open fields in 1863, with thick timber growing mostly right along the creek. Here, on gently rising ground and in the shelter of the timber, Wilder's men took up a position that gave them a good field of fire across the creek.

What Happened

On September 18 Wilder's brigade of mounted infantry was part of the Union screening force covering the crossing of Chickamauga Creek north of the Army of the Cumberland's main body. The several hours' delay in the Confederate advance that was gained by the determined stands here and at Reed's Bridge was crucial in allowing the Army of the Cumberland to avoid being cut off from Chattanooga.

Alexander's Bridge in those days was a rickety wooden

structure, and some of Wilder's men tore up the deck planks to build a small breastwork astride the road near where you stand. They put up a remarkable fight. The Confederates of *Liddell's* division attacked from 10:00 A.M. to 4:30 P.M. and managed to secure a crossing only after fellow Confederates, moving down from the bridgehead at Reed's Bridge, came up on the flank and rear of Wilder's brigade. Wilder destroyed the bridge and then made good his escape with most of his brigade intact.

Analysis

Wilder's success was made possible by the strength of his position (in contrast to the weak position on the west bank of the Chickamauga at Reed's Bridge), the very high morale of his men, and the heavy firepower of his Spencer Repeating Rifles. The Spencer had the same range and lethality as ordinary Civil War rifles, but gave from seven to ten times the rate of fire, thus multiplying the strength of Wilder's relatively small force.

Vignette

Years after the war was over, Capt. Joseph *Cumming,* one of the Confederates who had attacked the bridge, enjoyed needling his Northern friend Col. John T. Wilder. "He was disposed to take all things seriously," *Cumming* explained of Wilder, "and when I would 'start something' by remarking casually, 'General, when you and I opened the battle of Chickamauga, and we whipped you down there at Alexander Bridge. . . .' He replied with heat: 'I whipped you!' 'Why then,' I asked, 'Did you run away and leave the bridge?' 'I didn't run away. I destroyed the bridge and then moved off to whip some more of you at another place.' There was much truth in the old fighter's statement."

TO RETURN TO THE MAIN TOUR
Turn around and drive back in the direction from which you came on ALEXANDER'S BRIDGE ROAD, past the intersection of VINIARD-ALEXANDER ROAD, a total of 0.5 mile to JAY'S MILL ROAD. *Bear right. Proceed* past the intersection of BROTHERTON ROAD a total of 1.1 miles to REED'S BRIDGE ROAD. *Turn left. Proceed* just under 0.9 mile to the parking area on the right. Carefully cross the road and walk to the cannons. Turn to stop 1.

TO CONTINUE WITH THE SECONDARY TOUR
Turn around and drive back the way you came about 0.7 mile to JAY'S MILL ROAD. *Turn right. Proceed* not quite 1.0 mile to BROTHERTON ROAD. *Turn right. Proceed* about 0.3 mile and park in the turnout on the left near the sign pointing toward "Bragg's Headquarters." Turn to optional excursion 3.

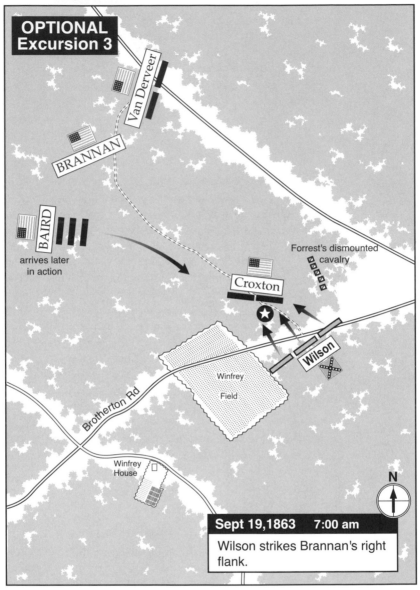

OPTIONAL
Excursion 3

Van Derveer

BRANNAN

BAIRD

arrives later
in action

Forrest's dismounted
cavalry

Croxton

Wilson

Winfrey
Field

Brotherton Rd

Winfrey
House

N

Sept 19,1863   7:00 am
Wilson strikes Brannan's right
flank.

OPTIONAL EXCURSION 3   Woods West of Jay's Mill   7:00 A.M., September 19

Wilson's Attack

Directions   Walk about 30 yards farther along the left side of the road to the vicinity of a trail-junction marker on the other side of the road. One trail leaves the road here to your left and two different trails leave it on your right. Turn right and face across the road (due north), toward the trail-junction marker for the left (red-blazed) trail.

Orientation   The Federal line ran roughly parallel to the trail in front of you, but its nearest flank (the right flank) was about 100 yards down the trail. The Union soldiers were facing to your right. The attack by Col. Claudius C. *Wilson's* Confederates jumped off behind you and moved in the direction you are now facing. The Confederate line was more or less parallel to the road here.

What Happened   When Brannan initially drove back *Forrest's* cavalry, he halted with his line running along the crest of a gentle ridge. The trail in front of you follows that crest. Brannan's left flank, at the far end of his line, just touched Reed's Bridge Road (at stop 1). This trail, of course, did not exist then, but the woods were much more open, allowing about 50 to 150 yards', visibility.

Forrest called for infantry support, received two brigades of Maj. Gen. William H. T. *Walker's* corps, and immediately hurled them into the fight. Brannan's left flank held, but here on his right, *Wilson's* Georgia brigade formed a line roughly parallel to the road beside which you are now standing and advanced through this position in the direction you are now facing. As the Confederate line passed the point where you are now standing, they might well have gotten their first glimpse of Brannan's right flank, about 100 yards ahead. This flank attack broke Brannan's right brigade, Croxton's, and forced it back some distance before it could stem the Confederate advance.

Now it was Thomas's turn to react, sending in another division under Brig. Gen. Absalom Baird. Baird turned the tables on the Confederates, flanking them and driving them back in disorder before himself being flanked by additional Confederate reinforcements (Brig. Gen. St. John R. *Liddell's* division of *Walker's* corps). This seesaw battle raged back and forth through these woods until about noon, with neither side gaining a clear advantage. As additional troops on each side moved up to join the battle, the fighting tended to spread southward (as you will observe at the next few stops).

Analysis   The key feature in the terrain of this part of the battlefield was the forest, but it was different from the forest that covers this ground today. General Thomas described this area as covered with woods so thick that in some places visibility was reduced to as little as 50 yards. Today it would be difficult in most places to see half that far. In the nineteenth century Americans allowed their hogs, cattle, and goats to graze in the woods, keeping the underbrush much reduced. As a result, many of the regiments that fought on this part of the field reported sighting the enemy and opening fire at ranges of 100 to 150 yards.

What did all this mean for the fighting that took place here? First, significant fighting could take place (something that would be all but impossible in the thickets that now cover this ground), but the woods changed the nature of that fighting. Engagements would occur within ranges of less than 150 yards, often much less. That meant they would be short, bloody, and more favorable to the attacker than Civil War combat usually was. It also meant that the exact location and orientation of the enemy's line of battle would not be known by commanders until their troops became engaged. This is what led to the remarkable series of devastating flank attacks. Defending units had almost no way of anticipating the precise direction of the next attack–and changing front to meet it–until too late. As a result, almost each additional unit that either side sent into the fight in this sector succeeded in flanking and routing at least some portion of the enemy line already established here. That made for a vicious struggle that raged to and fro over this area for hours.

Further Reading   Cozzens, *This Terrible Sound*, 125–38; Woodworth, *A Deep Steady Thunder*, 33–38.

TO RETURN TO THE MAIN TOUR
Proceed straight ahead about 0.4 mile to Winfrey Field. Park in the unimproved turnout on the right just before leaving the field. Turn to stop 2.

TO CONTINUE WITH THE SECONDARY TOUR
If you would like to explore the ground over which *Wilson's* and later *Govan's* and *Walthall's* Confederates battled Brannan's and Baird's Federals, you can make a 0.6-mile hike on the red-blazed trail that begins across the road from you. Turn to optional excursion 4, Woods West of Jay's Mill. If you are following the secondary tour of optional excursions, this is your next stop.

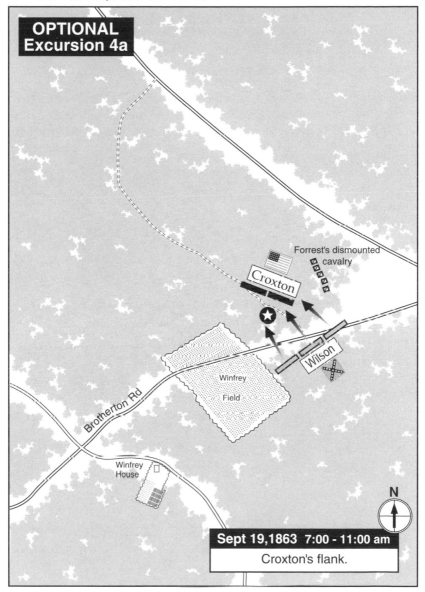

**OPTIONAL
Excursion 4a**

Forrest's dismounted
cavalry

Croxton

Winfrey
Field

Brotherton Rd

Wilson

Winfrey
House

N

Sept 19,1863 7:00 - 11:00 am
Croxton's flank.

OPTIONAL EXCURSION 4

Woods West of Jay's Mill   7:00–11:00 A.M., September 19

The First Phase of the Battle

Excursion Stop 4a   Croxton's Flank

Directions   Walk along the trail about 100 yards to the monument to the 74th Indiana, about 15 yards to the right of the trail up a small side trail. As you walk, you will be following the line of advance of *Wilson's* brigade, following much the same route a Confederate soldier would have except that a double line of men would have stretched out on either side of him through the open woods.

Orientation

Face toward the monument. You are near the right flank of Croxton's line, held by the 74th Indiana, and facing in the same direction his soldiers faced. The flanking attack described in the previous excursion approached from your right.

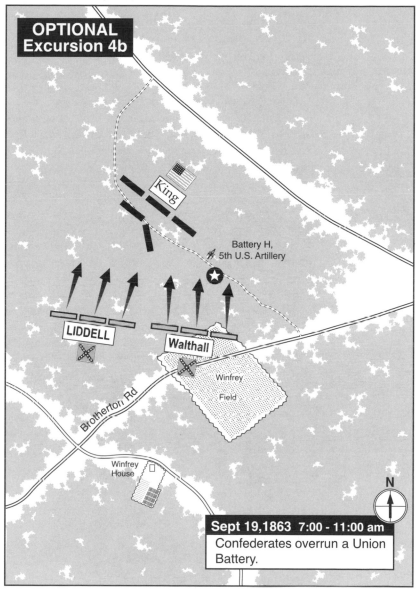

Excursion Stop 4b   Battery H, 5th U.S. Artillery

Directions

Continue walking another 370 yards to the monument and cannon representing Battery H, 5th U.S. Artillery, a few yards to the right of the trail. In doing so you will be continuing along the line of Croxton's brigade. For reasons that will appear shortly, these cannon face the opposite direction from that in which Battery H fired when it first deployed here. Face in the opposite direction of that in which the guns are pointing.

Orientation

You are near the left flank of Croxton's position, but Battery H arrived later, after Croxton had withdrawn, and occupied this position in support of Baird's division.

What Happened

After *Wilson* had driven in Croxton's brigade, Thomas sent Baird's division to come up and support Brannan on the right. Baird, along with Van Derveer's and John M. Connell's brigades of Brannan's division, drove *Wilson* back and halted near here. Battery H took up its position here, between Baird's two front-line brigades, Brig. Gen. John H. King's brigade of Regular U.S. Army regiments on your left (north) and Col. Benjamin Scribner's brigade several hundred yards to your right (south of here), near Winfrey Field. The action there is described at stop 2.

Bragg countered by sending in the division of Brig. Gen. St. John R. *Liddell*. Advancing from the south, it routed Scribner's brigade and then approached this position from your right and right rear. The Federal troops here never had a chance, and the battery was captured. The Confederates tried to turn the guns on their former owners, and that probably explains the orientation of the present commemorative cannon.

General J. M. Brannan, from a photograph taken in May 1865.
BLCW 3:660

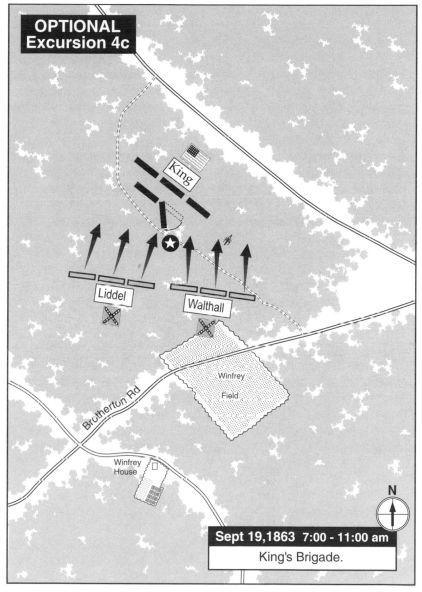

OPTIONAL Excursion 4c

King

Liddel

Walthall

Winfrey Field

Brotherton Rd

Winfrey House

N

Sept 19,1863   7:00 - 11:00 am

King's Brigade.

Excursion Stop 4c   King's Brigade

Directions

Continue another 85 yards to the monument for King's brigade, just to the right of the path. Face toward the monument.

Orientation

You are now at the position where King's brigade was struck in flank around 10:00 A.M. on the morning of the nineteenth.

What Happened   King and his officers tried to angle the brigade's right back–
roughly to your right rear–but Confederates were advancing
from that direction and still flanked the new line. Caught in
a hopeless position, the brigade went to pieces, losing hun-
dreds of prisoners.

Trooper of the Virginia Cavalry. One battalion of Virginia
cavalry, Edmundson's, par-
ticipated in the Chickamauga
campaign. BLCW 2:271

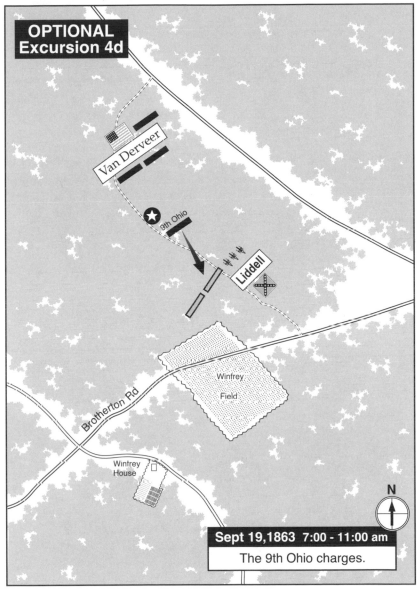

OPTIONAL Excursion 4d

Van Derveer

9th Ohio

Liddell

Winfrey Field

Brotherton Rd

Wintrey House

N

Sept 19,1863 7:00 - 11:00 am

The 9th Ohio charges.

Excursion Stop 4d The 9th Ohio

Directions

Another half-mile of walking along the trail would take you to Van Derveer's first position, stop 1. To continue with this excursion, turn around and walk back the way you came. About 50 yards from King's Monument you will come to the small stone monument to the 9th Ohio, just to the left of the path. Stand near the monument and face down the path in the direction toward which you have just been walking.

Orientation   You are facing in the same direction the men of the 9th Ohio faced as they charged.

What Happened   After Baird's division was routed, Brannan's division turned and struck southward to restore the Union front in this sector. As Van Derveer's brigade advanced from behind you in the direction you are now facing, the 9th Ohio, a regiment of Cincinnati Germans, launched one of its trademark impetuous bayonet charges. Partially from the vigor of their charge and partially because Van Derveer's whole brigade had now turned the tables on the Confederates and was advancing on *their* flank, the charge was a resounding success, sending *Liddell's* soldiers fleeing headlong and recapturing the guns of Battery H, 5th U.S., which you will pass again as you continue your return along the trail.

Confederate Types in 1862. BLCW 1:548

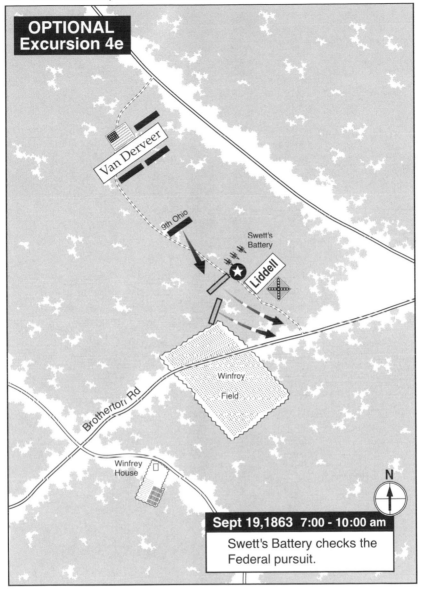

OPTIONAL
Excursion 4e

Van Derveer

9th Ohio

Swett's
Battery

Liddell

Winfroy
Field

Brotherton Rd

Winfrey
House

N

Sept 19,1863 7:00 - 10:00 am

Swett's Battery checks the
Federal pursuit.

**Excursion Stop 4e   The Warren Mississippi Light Artillery
(*Swett's* Battery)**

Directions   Continue along the trail back toward your starting point for
about 230 yards to the Park Service tablet commemorating
the Warren Mississippi Light Artillery (*Swett's* Battery), about
15 yards to the left of the trail. Stand near the tablet and face
toward it.

What Happened   *Swett's* Battery was attached to *Liddell's* division but had been unable to keep up with its rapid advance over wooded terrain as it pursued Baird's routed division. When the tables were turned, however, *Liddell's* division retreated over the ground on which you are now standing. *Swett's* Battery, which had trailed along behind, deployed here and helped check the Federal pursuit.

TO RETURN TO THE MAIN TOUR

Continue along the trail until you return to where you parked your car. *Proceed straight ahead* about 0.4 mile to Winfrey Field. Park in the unimproved turnout on the right just before leaving the field. Turn to stop 2.

TO CONTINUE WITH THE SECONDARY TOUR

Continue along the trail until you return to where you parked your car. *Proceed straight ahead* about 0.4 mile to Winfrey Field. Park in the unimproved turnout on the right just before leaving the field. Walk to the right (relative to the direction you have just been driving) along the edge of the field to the Baldwin Monument, another of those cannonball pyramids. Turn to optional excursion 5, Winfrey Field.

Saving a Gun. BLCW 4:293

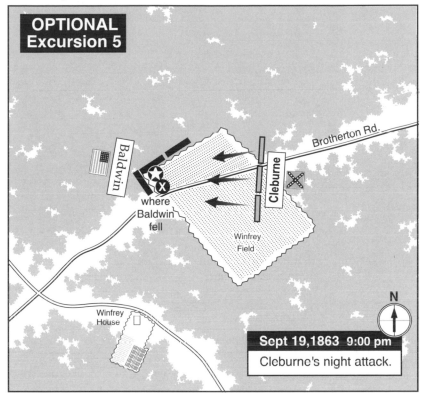

OPTIONAL
Excursion 5

Baldwin

Cleburne

Brotherton Rd.

where
Baldwin
fell

Winfrey
Field

N

Winfrey
House

Sept 19,1863 9:00 pm

Cleburne's night attack.

OPTIONAL EXCURSION 5   Winfrey Field   9:00 P.M., September 19

Cleburne's Night Attack

Orientation

Stand near the Baldwin Monument and face the open field with your back to the tree line along which you have just been walking. You are standing just in front of the position of the Union line on the evening of the nineteenth. It ran along the tree line behind you, where soldiers had piled dead branches and rocks along a rail fence to make a crude breastwork. At the corner of the field on your left, the line angled to follow the tree line and its convenient rail fence. This sector was held by Col. Philemon Baldwin's brigade, the left brigade of Johnson's division, whose lines ran off through the woods to your right rear. Baird was to the left and rear of Johnson. The Confederates of *Cleburne's* division advanced diagonally across the field more or less directly toward you from your right front.

What Happened

This was one of the most confused incidents of the battle. At dusk on September 19, *Polk* decided to launch the fresh division of Maj. Gen. Patrick R. *Cleburne* in a night attack against the Federals of Johnson's and Baird's divisions around Winfrey Field. Thomas had already decided to pull both divisions back from this exposed position to a more compact and defensible line around Kelly Field. The Union brigade commanders had just received the order to withdraw when *Cleburne's* Confederates came out of the gathering darkness. There was nothing to do but stay and fight if they could.

What followed was a confused affair in which "friendly fire" casualties were about as common as the intentional sort. Each side blazed away at the other with desperate energy, and night magnified the intensity of the conflict in the minds of the participants to the point that many of them would later insist this was the most furious conflict in their experience. The Confederates got on the right flank of the 1st Ohio, just to your right, and drove it back. Baldwin, trying to rally his men here, was fatally shot. The Confederates swept on over this ground, leaving the 5th Kentucky (Union) cut off on your left. By that time darkness was so deep that friend and foe could be distinguished only by the direction in which they shot. The 5th made off at double-quick time, dreading a Confederate volley until finally realizing that the Confederates had mistaken them for fellow Southerners. The bad side, of course, was that their Union comrades did the same, and another Union regiment gave them a volley. That made the Kentuckians all the more anxious to get to the rear, and they quickened their pace. Their Union comrades, seeing these "Confederates" who only charged faster when fired on, also set out for the rear. Meanwhile, some members of the 5th turned and gave the real Confederates a volley. These men, thinking they were receiving fire from a "Confederate" unit, gave up their pursuit and took cover.

Elsewhere along the line the struggle was confused and deadly and accomplished little. The Federals eventually made good their withdrawal to the Kelly Field perimeter, and *Cleburne's* men were left in possession of the ground and the numerous dead.

Analysis

A night march might be practical for a Civil War army, but night combat was not. Rarely was a decisive tactical result achieved in darkness, and even then it was a very exceptional case indeed in which the side that gained the tactical advantage was able to follow up its success in any significant way. This night action produced no effect but to lengthen the casualty lists and to disrupt *Cleburne's* division so that it was unable to participate effectively in the vastly more important assault the next morning.

Vignette   The next morning a Confederate soldier who had been temporarily detailed to duty in the rear passed over this ground on his way to rejoin his regiment. In his diary he described the appalling carnage that daylight revealed: "I had to pass over the ground where Cleburne had fought the evening before. The dead of both sides were lying thick over the ground where six Federal soldiers had been killed from behind one small tree, and where eight horses were lying dead harnessed to a Napoleon gun. Men and horses were lying so thick over the field, one could hardly walk for them. I even saw a large black dog lying mangled by a grape[shot]."

Further Reading   Cozzens, *This Terrible Sound*, 263–79.

TO RETURN TO THE MAIN TOUR
Proceed 0.2 mile to ALEXANDER'S BRIDGE ROAD. *Turn left. Proceed* past JAY'S MILL ROAD and VINIARD-ALEXANDER ROAD total of almost 1.5 miles to Alexander's Bridge. Park in the paved turnout on the right just before the bridge and then walk across it to the other side. Turn to stop 8.

TO CONTINUE WITH THE SECONDARY TOUR
Return to your vehicle and *continue driving* in the direction you were before for about another 1.3 miles to LA FAYETTE ROAD. *Turn right and then immediately left* on DYER ROAD. *Proceed* a little over 0.2 mile to GLENN-KELLY ROAD. *Turn right. Proceed* just over 0.5 mile to the parking area for the South Carolina Monument on your left. Walk along the path that follows the edge of the woods uphill and then along the gravel road, still going uphill toward the large monument that you see ahead of you. The total walk is about 300 yards. Follow the gravel road a few yards as it curves to the left near the crest. Turn to optional excursion 6, South Carolina Monument.

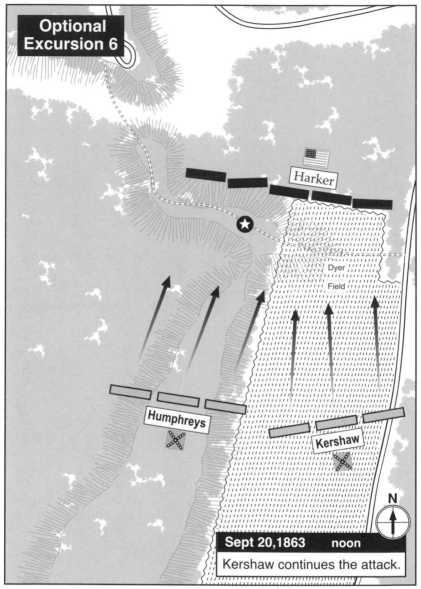

Optional Excursion 6

Harker

Dyer Field

Humphreys

Kershaw

N

Sept 20,1863   noon

Kershaw continues the attack.

OPTIONAL EXCURSION 6   South Carolina Monument   noon, September 20

Harker's Stand

Directions

Face back toward GLENN-KELLY ROAD (on which you have just been driving).

Orientation

The Federal position ran roughly from a little behind you down to where your vehicle is parked. The Confederates advanced across the field from your right.

What Happened   After taking most of the guns of the massed batteries on the
ridge to your right, the men of *Law's* division had little leisure
to savor the victory. They were soon under fire by a Union brigade advancing from the north and taking up a position
along the rail fence on the northern edge of Dyer Field. This
time it was the Confederates' turn to run, and *Law's* division
dropped back all the way to Dyer Road. Now, however, *Longstreet's* deep column of attack paid off again. Coming up in
support of *Law* were two brigades of Maj. Gen. Lafayette
McLaws's division, also of the Army of Northern Virginia, and
commanded in *McLaws's* absence by Brig. Gen. Joseph *Kershaw*.
As *Hood* eagerly brought these new troops into action, he was
shot in the right leg. When he was carried off toward the field
hospital and eventual amputation, he was still repeating, "Go
ahead, and keep ahead of everything."

   Kershaw, however, was equal to the crisis. Facing his fresh
troops to the north, *Kershaw* brought his two-to-one numerical superiority to bear on the Federals behind the fence, who
grudgingly fell back toward the high ground in Snodgrass
Field (to your left, beyond the woods).

Analysis   The Union brigade that drove *Law* out of the northern end
of the field and then took up a position here belonged to
Col. Charles G. Harker of Wood's division. Having cleared the
attack area before disaster struck, it was intact, and Wood
led it back to try to contain the Confederate breakthrough.
He was ultimately unsuccessful, but his alert and resolute
action—and the hard fighting of Harker's men—won much-
needed time for other troops to consolidate a defensive position on Snodgrass Hill and Horseshoe Ridge.

Vignette   As *Kershaw's* brigades advanced to the attack, Harker's brigade fell silent. Ahead of them the Confederates saw a long
line of blue uniforms, studded with eight color-bearers who
stood boldly erect and vigorously waved four United States
flags and four state banners. What the puzzled Confederates
probably interpreted as bravado was in fact nothing of the
sort, for the Federals were much more puzzled, believing that
they too saw in front of them a long line of blue uniforms
studded with flags that, "both in color and size, appeared in
the distance to resemble the brigade and division headquarters flags of McCook's corps." The Federals here had not yet
fully grasped the magnitude of the disaster that had befallen
Davis and Sheridan and hoped those divisions might even
now be moving up to support them. Thus the Army of Northern Virginia soldiers, with nattier uniforms and different pattern battle flags than their western counterparts, confused

the Union officers. Harker later described his dilemma: "The idea of firing upon our own troops was a most horrible one to me, yet if perchance they should be rebels, valuable time was being lost to me, and they would take advantage of it." As Lt. Charles Clark, Company H, 125th Ohio, recalled, "Just when we ought to have poured the entire contents of our cartridge boxes into those moving battalions as rapidly as possible . . . orders were given to cease firing and keep the flags well up." The Confederates soon removed any doubts as to their identity by opening fire, and the fight was on again.

Further Reading   Cozzens, *This Terrible Sound*, 406–16; Woodworth, *A Deep Steady Thunder*, 86–89.

Further Exploration You can walk the route that *Kershaw's* troops followed as they pursued Harker's retreating Federals and then assaulted Horseshoe Ridge. If you do, you can complete stops 18 and 19 on foot and then walk back to your car where it is now parked. To the right rear of the South Carolina Monument (nearest the corner with the white "Erected 1901" stone in it) a trail leads into the woods. Follow it as it leads down through a valley and then starts up again, coming to a gravel road. This is the Vittatoe Road, so named for a farmer whose house stood in 1863 at its end several hundred yards to your left. Follow the trail on the other side of the Vittatoe Road up the steep slope of Horseshoe Ridge, continuing to follow the route over which Confederate soldiers charged. The Union defenders were ranged along the crest above you. You will emerge among the monuments commemorating Van Derveer's brigade. To your right is a monument depicting several soldiers holding a flag. Walk to it, face the way the bronze soldiers are facing, and turn to stop 19. Note: Since the action discussed in stops 18 and 19 is simultaneous, you can do stop 19 first and then do stop 18 as you continue a loop that will take you back to your car.

TO RETURN TO THE MAIN TOUR
Proceed straight ahead about 0.2 mile to VITTATOE ROAD. *Turn left. Proceed* 0.1 mile to a fork in the road. *Take the right fork*, SNODGRASS ROAD, and *proceed* 0.1 mile to the Snodgrass House. Park in the turnout on the right, near the Snodgrass House, and walk down the open, monument-lined ridge to the monument with a statue of a tiger on top of it. Turn to stop 18.

TO CONTINUE WITH THE SECONDARY TOUR
Return to your vehicle and continue driving in the same direction you last were (since Glenn-Kelly Road is one-way, you

don't have any choice). *Proceed* about 0.1 mile to VITTATOE ROAD. *Turn left. Proceed* 0.2 mile to a fork in the road. *Take the right fork,* SNODGRASS ROAD, *and proceed* about 0.2 mile to a parking area located at the terminus of this road. Walk up the ridge, keeping to the cleared area, which will gradually narrow to the width of a footpath. The path descends a bit to the 21st Ohio Monument, which is misplaced. The extreme left flank of the regiment would probably have been a little farther up the path yet, and the regiment's main stand was made at the top of the next rise (still following the path), where you will find a small clearing and various monuments to units of Steedman's division. As you walk to this position, remember that the Confederates were advancing up the hill from your left, while Steedman's reinforcements came up from your right. Turn to optional excursion 7, Upper Horseshoe Ridge.

Major General
J. B. Kershaw.
BLCW 3:330

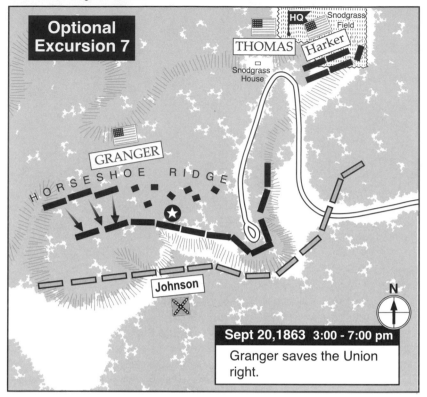

OPTIONAL EXCURSION 7

Upper Horseshoe Ridge   3:00–7:00 P.M., September 20

Granger Saves the Union Right

Directions   Stand near the 22nd Michigan Monument and to the left of
                      the direction you were just walking.

Orientation   You are standing near the center of the line of the 21st Ohio,
                      facing as its soldiers did. The Confederates charged up the
                      hill toward you. For several hours this was the extreme right
                      of the Union line.

What Happened   The key struggle occurred on the extreme Federal right.
                      There the 539 officers and men of the 21st Ohio made one of
                      the truly heroic defensive stands of the Civil War, compa-
                      rable to the more famous stand of the 20th Maine at Gettys-
                      burg. They were the flank, and if they gave way, Thomas's
                      whole position was gone. Seven of their ten companies were
                      equipped with Colt Revolving Rifles, which boosted their fire-
                      power. They needed all the help they could get as they fought
                      on against superior numbers, repulsing one Confederate

assault after another. The lieutenant colonel commanding went down; a major took over. The line stretched thin as the regiment endeavored to prevent the Confederates from getting around their right. Then it could stretch no more, and the Southerners gained the ridgetop still further to the right and came in on the Ohioans' flank. The two right flank companies swung back to face them. It seemed that the last desperate moment had come.

Then from the woods behind the struggling Ohioans came a deep, loud cheer rising from 450 throats, and the long blue battle line of the 22nd Michigan surged over the crest, through the Ohioans' lines, and into the surprised Confederates, hurling them back down the hill. The Michigan troops were the left flank regiment of a full division of fresh Union troops just reaching the field at that crucial moment. The division was that of Brig. Gen. James Blair Steedman, part of the Army of the Cumberland's small Reserve Corps under Maj. Gen. Gordon Granger. Though much hard fighting remained to be done and many of Steedman's regiments— including the 22nd Michigan—would lose half their numbers in the struggle to hold the ridge, their timely arrival had made possible the continued Union stand on Snodgrass Hill and Horseshoe Ridge.

Analysis

Aside from the incredible tenacity of the soldiers themselves, the key factor in saving the Union right flank from a true disaster was the exercise of wise initiative on the part of Granger. His Reserve Corps had been stationed several miles north of the battlefield, and his orders were to remain there. Nevertheless, as the day wore on and he heard nothing from Rosecrans while he did hear a great deal of firing to the south, he concluded that a great battle was in progress and that all of the army ought to be present. Acting without orders and solely on his own initiative, he did what good generals are always supposed to do and marched to the sound of the guns. His arrival could not have been more timely or more needed, particularly since he brought a large supply of rifle ammunition, badly needed by Thomas's hard-fighting men on Snodgrass Hill and Horseshoe Ridge.

Vignette

Lt. Wilson Vance of the 21st Ohio described the desperate nature of the struggle as his regiment hung on grimly before the arrival of Steedman's division. "Our assailants," Vance wrote, "seemed to understand that our frail line was all they had to overcome to reach the rear and very heart of the horseshoe formation. There was that peculiar fierceness in the manner of the assault that men show when they realize that the supreme opportunity has presented itself, and are determined not to let it slip. And our boys could do nothing but set their teeth and fight, as for their lives."

Further Reading Cozzens, *This Terrible Sound*, 417–521; Woodworth, *A Deep Steady Thunder*, 92–97.

This concludes the secondary tour of optional excursions.

View of Lookout Mountain from the hill to the north, which was General Hooker's position during the Battle of the Mountain, November 24, 1863. BLCW3:694

Chattanooga

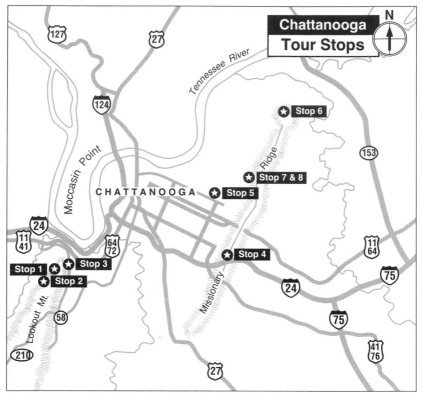

Introduction

In many ways, Chattanooga's battlefields are disappointing, confusing, and frustrating to visit. Unlike Chickamauga, Chattanooga offers no large areas preserved more or less as they were in 1863. The battle sites that the visitor may view profitably today are few, scattered, and surrounded by an urban environment that is at best irritating and in several cases downright threatening. Traffic will obviously have to be endured, and a good amount of city driving will have to be done to get to some of the sites. Roads are narrow and confusing, and the experience can be frustrating. Visitors sometimes feel, upon reaching a site, that they have battled an extreme amount of vexatious city traffic to arrive at an extremely small piece of preserved battlefield.

If that doesn't deter you, Chattanooga is not without its rewards. It was in some ways one of the most dramatic battles of the war because it was played out in the mammoth natural amphitheater of the Chattanooga Basin. Towering mountains all around provided spectacular scenery, dramatic stages for action, and breathtaking vantage points for observation. The modern visitor can still benefit from many of those factors. As one of the participants wrote, "When history shall have recorded the thrilling tragedies enacted here, when poets shall have illuminated every hilltop and mountain peak with the glow of their imagination, when the novelist shall have given it a population from his fertile brain—what place can be more attractive to the traveler?"

The Siege of Chattanooga: September–November 1863

After the battle of Chickamauga, Rosecrans's army retreated into Chattanooga, where *Bragg* virtually besieged it by occupying the heights that dominated it from the south (Lookout Mountain and Missionary Ridge) and also controlled the only practical route by which supplies could enter the city–the Tennessee River gorge west of Chattanooga. Reacting to this desperate situation, Union authorities took several important steps: Maj. Gen. Joseph Hooker with 23,000 reinforcements was dispatched by rail from the Army of the Potomac in Virginia to Stevenson, Alabama, just west of Chattanooga on the Tennessee River. Maj. Gen. William T. Sherman was dispatched overland from Mississippi with 20,000 men of the Army of the Tennessee, recent captors of Vicksburg. Most important, Maj. Gen. Ulysses S. Grant was given command of all Union forces between the Appalachians and the Mississippi and sent to Chattanooga to take command. Grant promptly sacked Rosecrans, replacing him with Thomas, and implemented a plan Rosecrans's staff had devised for reopening a supply line. Having successfully accomplished this, Grant prepared to deal with *Bragg*.

Bragg was handicapped by the poor performance and uncooperativeness of James *Longstreet* and by the near mutiny of many of his other generals. Confederate president Jefferson *Davis* tried to remedy the problem by visiting the Army of Tennessee and finally allowing *Bragg* to take firm action against the mutinous generals. *Polk* was transferred, *Hill* demoted and transferred, *Buckner* effectively demoted without any change in nominal rank. *Hindman* escaped only because he had been badly wounded at Chickamauga. Yet even these steps proved to be too little, too late. The Army of Tennessee's command system tottered toward complete breakdown.

Once Grant had opened his supply line (the famed "Cracker Line"), thus defeating the Confederate strategy of starving the Federals out of Chattanooga, *Bragg* had to come up with a new plan. This was to clear East Tennessee, reopen the rail line to Virginia, then draw supplies from that direction while moving around Grant's left (eastern) flank and threatening the Union supply line. At *Davis's* suggestion, the first step, clearing East Tennessee, was to be carried out by *Longstreet's* command, so as to keep that body handy to *Lee* in Virginia. Once sent off to East Tennessee, however, *Longstreet* proved slow and ineffective and had not, as *Bragg* had planned, completed his part of the operation before Sherman joined Grant.

Thus *Bragg* was left at a moderate disadvantage in numbers when on November 23 Grant launched the battle of Chattanooga.

STOP 1   **Grant Opens the "Cracker Line"**

Stop 1a   Confederate Artillery   September–October

Directions

Turn left from the Chickamauga Visitor Center parking lot. *Proceed* not quite 1.1 miles to BATTLEFIELD PARKWAY (Georgia Route 2). *Turn left. Proceed* 4.7 miles to GEORGIA ROUTE 193. *Turn right. Proceed* 4.2 miles to OCHS HIGHWAY (Tennessee Route 58; NOTE: When you cross the Georgia-Tennessee line, Georgia Route 193 becomes Tennessee Route 17). *Turn very sharply left* and follow OCHS HIGHWAY up the steep mountainside. Once you reach the top of the mountain, you may see signs directing you to "Point Park." If you wish, you may follow these signs as they lead you through the winding residential neighborhoods of the town of Lookout Mountain. Or you may follow the directions below.

Continue on OCHS HIGHWAY a total of about 2.2 miles to OCHS HIGHWAY EXTENSION. If you miss Ochs Highway Extension, *don't panic!* There are plenty of signs on the mountaintop directing you to Point Park. Simply follow them. You'll get there without too much extra mileage. If, however, you do catch OCHS HIGHWAY EXTENSION, *turn right* on it. *Proceed* about 0.6 mile to SOUTH FOREST AVENUE. *Turn right. Proceed* slightly over 0.1 mile to SCENIC HIGHWAY. *Turn right. Proceed* just over 0.1 mile to HERMITAGE ROAD. *Turn left. Proceed* 1.1 miles (during which HERMITAGE ROAD changes its name to EAST BROW BOULEVARD) to Point Park, recognizable by its castlelike gateway. A small parking lot is located just behind the Visitor Center, adjacent to the entrance of the park. If it's full, you'll have to park along the street. Parking meters are ubiquitous and constantly patrolled. You'll want to allow *at least* 30 minutes. Carefully note the time you will need to be back to your car. Walk through the castlelike gateway and follow the paved walkway to your right until you come to the second pair of cannon pointing off the mountain. Stand near the cannon and face in the direction they do, overlooking the city of Chattanooga.

Orientation

The Army of the Cumberland was encamped around Chattanooga below. At that time, of course, the town of Chattanooga was *much* smaller than the modern-day city. A small town of hardly 2,000 peacetime inhabitants, the Chattanooga of 1863 scarcely occupied the area that is today downtown Chattanooga, where you see high-rise buildings near the Tennessee River. The Confederates held this mountain and emplaced their longest-ranged artillery pieces, the 10-pounder Parrot Rifles of *Garrity's* Alabama Battery, here. Note: The Park

Service tablet here represents *Garrity's* Battery, but the cannon are 12-pounder Napoleons of the type used by *Corput's* Georgia Battery, which occupied this position later.

What Happened

During the siege of Chattanooga, the Confederates tried their hand at shelling the Federals out of the town. The guns here were supposed to do the job. The result demonstrated the unsuitability of Civil War cannon for long-range bombardment. The cannon were at their best when firing canister against charging infantry, filling the role that machine guns did in World War I. They were at their worst when trying to do serious damage to an enemy in camp or in fortifications a long way off.

This was because their accuracy was insufficient and so was the lethality of the shells, in this case 10-pound iron cylinders with an explosive core of black powder. The artillerists' biggest handicap, however, was that they had no way of detonating their shells other than by the use of a simple gunpowder fuse, hand-cut by the gunner according to his estimate of the range. That the powder did not always burn at a constant rate only made matters worse. Consequently, some shells burst harmlessly far too early. Others burst late, after burying themselves in mud and thus smothering their meager explosive force. Still others never burst at all. Eventually the effort to bombard the Federals from the mountaintop was largely abandoned, and the long-range guns were replaced here by the shorter-ranged brass Napoleons of *Corput's* Georgia Battery (the bluish-colored cannon you now see).

Vignette

Though a Union officer wrote on September 25 that the "Rebel artillery on Lookout Mountain opened on us and made us hunt our holes," the Federals below soon got used to the shelling and came to realize that relatively few men were hurt by it. Ten days later, another Federal officer related the following account: "The enemy opened on us, at 11 A.M., from batteries located on the point of Lookout Mountain, and continued to favor us with cast iron in the shape of shell and solid shot until sunset. He did little damage, however; three men only were wounded, and these but slightly. A shell entered the door of a dog tent [pup tent], near which two soldiers of the Eighteenth Ohio were standing, and buried itself in the ground, when one of the soldiers turned very coolly to the other and said: 'There, see what you get by leaving your door open!'"

Further Reading

Sword, *Mountains Touched with Fire*, 96–98.

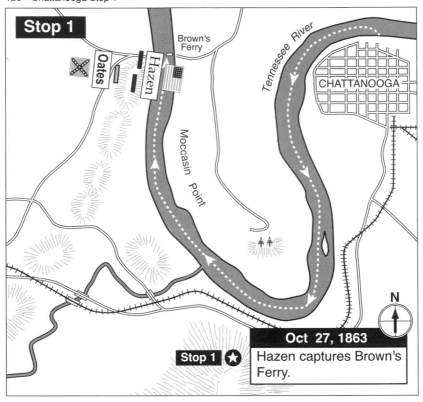

Stop 1b   Taking Brown's Ferry   October 27

Directions

Continue walking on the paved path along the edge of the park until you come to the sign pointing toward the Ochs Museum. Go down the steps to the museum. The museum itself offers little, but the view from the adjoining overlook is worth coming to Point Park to see. Stand near the middle of the overlook and look over Chattanooga and the surrounding area 1,400 feet below you.

Orientation

The large mountain on your left is Raccoon Mountain. Between it and you is Lookout Valley. The Tennessee River loops toward you, forming Moccasin Bend immediately in front of Lookout Mountain. Beyond it is the large mass of Walden's Ridge. To your right is Chattanooga, much larger than it was in 1863. Just beyond the visible part of Chattanooga, running diagonally to the right and beyond it and visible as a low, dark green line, is Missionary Ridge (which will seem much larger when you are on it). The Confederate line ran from the far end of Missionary Ridge, along the crest of the ridge, through the valley separating it from Lookout Mountain, around the lower slope of Lookout Mountain (below you and out of sight), and, in the form of a skirmish line, all the way across Lookout Valley to the lower slopes of Raccoon Mountain. The Army of the Cumberland was in Chattanooga (what is now downtown Chattanooga). Hooker with 10,000 men (the rest of his force was guarding the railroad connections between here and Nashville) was on the far side of Raccoon Mountain at Bridgeport, and Sherman's Army of the Tennessee was still further in that direction and, for the moment, out of the equation.

What Happened

The events involved in the opening of the "Cracker Line" occurred in the area of Moccasin Bend and Lookout Valley.

The problem for the Union high command was that the only good route to bring supplies into Chattanooga was through a gap in Raccoon Mountain to your left rear, then northward through Lookout Valley and around the base of Lookout Mountain, in front of and below you. The Confederates on Raccoon Mountain, in Lookout Valley, and on the lower slopes of Lookout Mountain itself closed that route to them. The only remaining route went a long and roundabout way over the execrable dirt roads of Walden's Ridge. Far too few supplies came in that way, and Grant proposed to do something about it.

In the predawn hours of October 27, a Federal landing party, using pontoons as boats and commanded by Brig. Gen. William B. Hazen, boldly floated down the Tennessee River and around Moccasin Bend under the noses of the Confederates on the lower slopes of Lookout. They made their landing at Brown's Ferry. If you look toward the far end of the land enclosed by Moccasin Bend, near the middle of the peninsula, you will see something that looks like an enormous swimming pool (it is in fact the city sewage treatment plant). Brown's Ferry crossed the river just to your left of that point.

The Federals then threw a pontoon bridge across the river at Brown's Ferry, connecting with a road they had built across the base (far end) of Moccasin Point. Confederate resistance was feeble, and supplies were soon flowing over the new, shorter, and far more practical route. The starving times in Chattanooga gradually came to an end.

Analysis

Several key factors contributed to this Federal success: an excellent plan devised by Rosecrans's chief engineer, Brig. Gen. William F. "Baldy" Smith; Grant's forceful decisiveness in putting that plan into prompt execution; and the weakness of the Confederate defense owing to the confusion of *Long-*

street, who commanded this sector. *Longstreet* did not realize the importance to the Federals of opening this supply line, and he expected them to strike elsewhere. Thus he left Lookout Valley and Raccoon Mountain, including the area around Brown's Ferry, fatally undermanned.

Further Reading   Sword, *Mountains Touched with Fire*, 112–22.

Hazen's men landing from pontoon boats at Brown's Ferry. BLCW 3:688

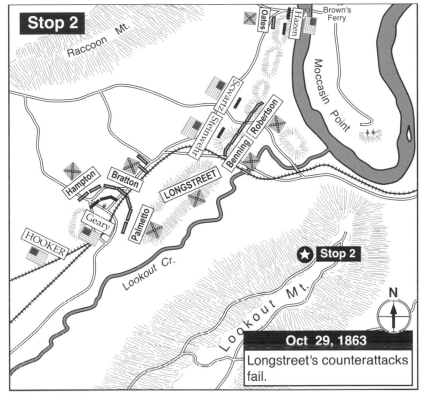

STOP 2

The Battle of Wauhatchie   October 29

Directions

The streets in the immediate vicinity of Point Park are all one-way, so you won't have much choice about which direction to start out. *Continue around the block* until you come to EAST BROW BOULEVARD. By this point it will no longer be one-way. *Turn right. Proceed* one block to RICHARDSON STREET. *Turn right. Proceed* two blocks to the point at which Richardson Street ends in a T-intersection with WEST BROW ROAD. *Turn left. Proceed* about 0.7 mile to Sunset Rock Park on your right. You will have to watch carefully for this one. All that will be visible to you from the road will be a small parking area – half a dozen spaces – set back among the trees and hedges of the comfortable community of Lookout Mountain. Walk down the trail from the parking area to Sunset Rock, an enormous outcropping on the side of the mountain. The trail is rough and rocky, but the view from Sunset Rock is spectacular.

Orientation

Below you lies Lookout Valley, stretching off to the southwest (your left). Opposite you is Raccoon Mountain. To your right, beyond the shoulder of Lookout Mountain itself, you can see Moccasin Bend of the Tennessee River. Now take a closer look at the terrain. To your left front, on the other side of the valley, the slope of Raccoon Mountain is gouged and scarred by an enormous rock quarry. Look just a little farther to the left and you'll see the sloping edge of the spur of the mountain into which the quarry was cut. A little farther to your left you'll see another sloping edge of a mountain. That's the southernmost extremity of Raccoon Mountain. The high ground you see beyond it is part of Sand Mountain. Between Raccoon and Sand Mountains lies Running Water Gap. If the day is clear and your eyes are sharp, you may just be able to discern the mouth of the gap. In the wall of Raccoon Mountain directly opposite you, you'll find it much easier to make out a valley running back into the range. That's Cummings Gap. Now let your eyes drop downward a little to the cleared and somewhat built-up area just this side of the gap. That's Wauhatchie. Still closer to you is a railroad. It was not located there in 1863. Instead both the railroad and the main highway ran side by side through Wauhatchie and then along the valley to your right until they reached two small but relatively prominent hills that rise about 150 feet from the middle of the valley floor on your right front. Road and railroad then passed between the hills (as a road and another railroad do today), angling toward the foot of Lookout Mountain and Chattanooga beyond. Another road continues on the far side of both hills and then along the far side of a row of smaller hills than run down the middle of the valley beyond and all the way to the banks of the Tennessee River at Brown's Ferry (which you viewed at the previous stop).

What Happened On October 28, Hooker's three divisions marched from Bridgeport and into Lookout Valley through Running Water Gap (in the distance on your left front). Then they turned down the valley (toward your right) and marched northward under ineffective shelling from Confederate cannon at the point of Lookout Mountain (see Chattanooga stop 1A), while both *Bragg* and *Longstreet* watched from this very point. Two of the divisions, the XI Corps, continued all the way to Brown's Ferry, but Hooker had the other, the XII Corps division of Brig. Gen. John W. Geary, halt at the crossroads of Wauhatchie, in hopes it could cover Cummings Gap, a vital part of the Cracker Line.

Bragg was deeply disturbed at the collapse of his strategy of starving the Federals out of Chattanooga and even more so at the arrival of Hooker's troops, which made restoration of the siege that much more difficult. *Longstreet*, though viewing the disproof of a previous pet theory of his to the effect that Hooker would get up on top of Lookout Mountain well to the south and then march along its crest, nevertheless affected his usual aplomb, asserting that control of Lookout Valley–and thus the only practical Union supply line–was unimportant.

Unconvinced, *Bragg* ordered *Longstreet*, whose sector this was, to get the Federals out of Lookout Valley and made ample forces available to him for the purpose. Instead, *Longstreet*, stubbornly insisting on the unimportance of the valley, chose to use only a single division in a night attack, October 28–29. It was a confused action that took place in two different locations in Lookout Valley in front of you and to your right front.

Longstreet ordered Brig. Gen. Micah *Jenkins* to attack the division at Wauhatchie, which he mistook for a wagon train with a few hundred guards. *Longstreet's* plan called for Brig. Gen. Evander M. *Law* to take two brigades and occupy the two hills (on your right front) that overlook the road between Wauhatchie and Brown's Ferry, to prevent the troops at the latter place from coming to the aid of those at Wauhatchie.

Law carried out his mission, successfully distracting a relieving column (the XI Corps) that Hooker rushed up the valley when he heard firing at Wauhatchie. *Jenkins*, despite fierce fighting, was unable to destroy Geary's comparable force–no surprise, since Civil War combat tended to favor the defender if other factors were anywhere near equal. *Jenkins* finally retired, and *Law* followed. The Cracker Line would stay open, unchallenged, for the remainder of the campaign, and the Confederates pulled their lines back to the flank of Lookout Mountain, the slopes to your lower right.

Vignette

One of the strangest stories to come out of this incident is that of the stampede of the Union mules. As the story goes, Union teamsters in Geary's wagon train, surprised by *Jenkins's* night attack, fled, leaving their mules. The animals then took fright and stampeded directly toward Confederate lines, disrupting them at a key moment of the attack.

The story is probably at least badly exaggerated, but one anonymous soldier of the 29th Ohio was inspired by it to parody Tennyson:

> *Half a mile, half a mile, half a mile onward,*
> *Right towards the Georgia troops, broke the two hundred.*
> *"Forward, the Mule Brigade,"*
> *"Charge for the Rebs!" they neighed;*
> *Straight for the Georgia troops broke the two hundred.*

And so on it went through five more stanzas.

Further Reading

Cozzens, *Shipwreck of Their Hopes*, 48–100; McDonough, *Chattanooga*, 49–94.

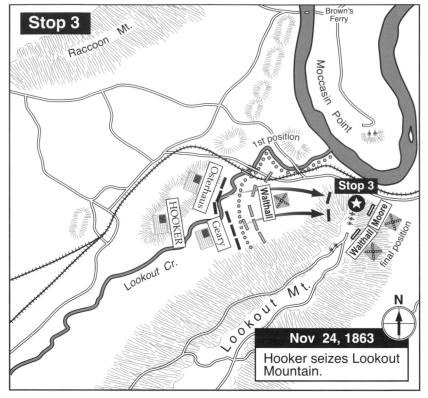

Stop 3

Raccoon Mt.

Moccasin Point

Brown's Ferry

1st position

Osterhaus

Walthall

Stop 3

HOOKER

Geary

Walthall | Moore

final position

Lookout Cr.

Lookout Mt.

N

Nov 24, 1863

Hooker seizes Lookout Mountain.

STOP 3   **"The Battle Above the Clouds"** November 24

Directions

Continue in the direction your were most recently driving on WEST BROW ROAD, following it around a sharp bend to the left, then going straight (even though West Brow later goes off to the right and the road you are traveling on becomes Sunset Road). About 0.8 mile from Sunset Rock you will come to BRAGG ROAD. *Turn right. Proceed* two blocks to SCENIC HIGHWAY. *Turn left. Proceed* 1.4 miles to the sign for CRAVENS HOUSE at UPPER CRAVENS TERRACE ROAD. (This intersection lacks a sign naming the road but does have a sign directing visitors to the Cravens House.) *Turn left. Proceed* 0.5 mile to the parking area at the Cravens House. *En route*, notice the markers and monuments denoting the final Confederate line, the limit of Union advance in the battle of Lookout Mountain, November 24. Walk to the tablet and guns in the open grassy area beside the Cravens House. Face in the direction the cannons are pointing, toward the tall monument on the other side of the grassy clearing.

Orientation

You are standing along one of many defensive lines the Confederates attempted to hold that day, facing as the Confederate soldiers faced. The Federals advanced directly toward your position along the side of the mountain in a line that stretched from the base of the "palisades" (the more or less vertical rocky walls near the mountain's summit) above you to well below you.

What Happened   Nearly a month after the opening of the Cracker Line, Grant was ready to take on *Bragg's* army. As a diversion from what he planned as his main thrust at the other end of the line, Grant permitted Hooker to try to take Lookout Mountain.

Hooker got his troops onto the western slopes of the mountain south of the area held by Confederate troops (out of sight around the bend of the mountainside in front of you and well to your left), then advanced northward toward the point of the mountain (here). Thus the battle was not fought by Union troops coming up the mountain at the defending Confederates but by Union troops moving along the side of the mountain against Confederates who had originally been deployed to face downhill. Confederate troops resisted but were driven back, around the point of the mountain, to this point.

This was to have been a main line of resistance in case the Confederates should be driven from the positions on the west side of the mountain, and the Southerners attempted to make a determined stand here. It was doomed almost from the outset. All the infantry available for defense here, *Walthall's* and *John C. Brown's* brigades, was considerably worse for the wear as a result of its treatment on the other side of the mountain. The exhausted and demoralized troops could offer only feeble resistance. That resistance was quickly ended when Union troops advancing along the base of the palisades (on your left) lapped around the left flank of the Confederates trying to hold this position and came down on the exposed flank from above. The position went to pieces, and the commander of the section of artillery here, having sent his horses to the rear, had no choice but to abandon his guns as the infantrymen fled.

The battle surged back along the eastern slope for about 300 yards behind you. There, gathering darkness, exhaustion, lack of ammunition, and the fact that the Confederates finally got a force of their own up to the foot of the palisades to stop the devastating Yankee flank attacks at last brought the Union advance to a halt.

Because a heavy fog veiled the mountain from the view of those in Chattanooga throughout most of the fight, it came to be called (and gained instant newspaper fame as) "the battle above the clouds."

Analysis

Once Hooker got onto the slope south of the Confederate position, advancing along the side of the slope against the Rebel flank, the Southern advantage in terrain was canceled. Confederate command problems prevented adequate reinforcements from reaching the defenders of the mountain, and Union superiority in numbers was decisive.

Vignette

While Hooker's troops fought for the mountain, most of the Federal army waited in suspense, listening to sounds of the battle to try to guess its course and hoping for an occasional glimpse of its progress when the fog would part. As resistance here at the Cravens House broke and Hooker's advancing troops surged past the house, they raised a mighty cheer that was heard and understood by their comrades below. One wrote, "Finally faint cheers came down to us from the mountain. It was the signal of victory and we took it up." Another recorded, "The glad cry spread from camp to camp and we listened to its echoes far up the majestic Tennessee River. We shook hands, we danced, we cried, we threw our hats in the air, and we shouted our victory again and again, as the faint voices above us came down." The next morning dawned clear, and the Federals in Chattanooga had cause to cheer again. "As the morning sun rose it discovered the national banner floating out in the mountain air from Lookout Point [Chattanooga stop 2], and the soldiery below caught up a shout from the regiment on the summit which rang through the crags and valleys and was borne to their comrades below, who were standing to arms behind the defenses of Chattanooga."

Further Reading

Cozzens, *Shipwreck of Their Hopes*, 159–204. McDonough, *Chattanooga*, 129–42.

Further Exploration

The Rifle Pits Trail trailhead is just across the parking area from the Cravens House. It's a pleasant walk following the route by which the Federals drove the Confederates back to the Cravens House, but you will need imagination to see rifle pits.

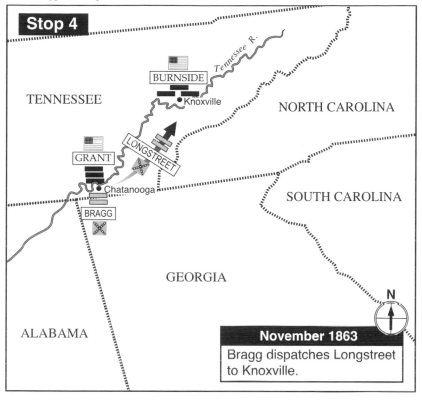

Stop 4

TENNESSEE

BURNSIDE

Tennessee R.

Knoxville

NORTH CAROLINA

GRANT

LONGSTREET

Chatanooga

SOUTH CAROLINA

BRAGG

GEORGIA

N

ALABAMA

November 1863

Bragg dispatches Longstreet
to Knoxville.

STOP 4   *Bragg's* **Strategic Problem**   October–November

Directions   *Drive back* along UPPER CRAVENS TERRACE ROAD 0.6 mile to
SCENIC HIGHWAY. *Turn left. Proceed* about 1.2 miles to STATE
ROUTE 318 (OLD WAUHATCHIE HIGHWAY). *Turn right. Proceed*
about 0.3 mile to CUMMINGS HIGHWAY (which also happens to
be U.S. Routes 11, 64, 41, and 72 and State Route 2). *Turn right.
Proceed* 2.5 miles (during which time the route numbers remain the same but the name changes to BROAD STREET) to
I-24. As you approach the interstate, follow the signs directing you to I-24 EAST. Take I-24 EAST 1.2 miles to U.S. Route 27
South–ROSSVILLE ROAD. Follow U.S. 27 South 2.9 miles to
SOUTH CREST ROAD, easily recognizable by the tall white column of the Iowa Monument at its intersection. *Turn left. Proceed* 3.3 miles to Bragg Reservation. *Turn right, then immediately
left* into the parking lot. *En route* you will be following the
route taken by Hooker's command on November 25 as it
crossed Chattanooga Valley to Rossville, ascended Rossville
Gap, and turned northward along the ridge about where you
turned onto Crest Road, helping to complete the Union victory on Missionary Ridge about which you will read in subsequent stops.

For now, however, walk toward the tall column of the Illinois Monument. As you do, you'll pass on your right a bronze tablet denoting *Bragg's* headquarters, located in a house that stood about here. Stand near the monument and face in the direction the nearby cannon are facing.

Orientation

Near this site in 1863 stood the house in which *Bragg* made his headquarters during the entire siege and battle of Chattanooga. You are now looking out over the city of Chattanooga. The growth is thicker on the other side of the road than it was in 1863, and it obscures the view of the city. Otherwise your perspective would be similar to *Bragg's* as he surveyed the town, the Federal army, and the strategic prospects.

What Happened

From this perspective, *Bragg* pondered the various problems he faced in trying to defeat the Union forces in Chattanooga. After *Longstreet's* failure to hold—and then to retake—the key positions on the left that would have continued to deny adequate supplies to the Federals in Chattanooga, *Bragg* had to come up with another solution. He did not leave a written record of his intentions, but everything he did seems to point to a plan to move around to the east of Grant's army and strike the Union lines of communication. A key first step toward carrying out that strategy was to remove a Union force under Ambrose Burnside that was currently holding Knoxville, Tennessee. Burnside's force was denying *Bragg* use of the key railroad into Virginia—which could be even more important if *Bragg* had to cast loose from his railroad supply line running back to Atlanta. From Knoxville, Burnside could also threaten *Bragg's* rear during the contemplated march around Grant.

To carry out the removal of Burnside from Knoxville, *Bragg* selected *Longstreet's* command, primarily at the suggestion of Confederate president Jefferson *Davis*, who in turn was under pressure from *Lee* to bring *Longstreet* and his divisions closer to Virginia as a step toward their early return to *Lee's* army. *Longstreet* was to move quickly, destroy Burnside's force or drive it out of East Tennessee, and either return to Chattanooga or else join *Bragg's* army as it marched north on the offensive. All of this was supposed to happen before Grant received substantial reinforcements then already known to be on the way.

Instead, *Longstreet* moved slowly and bombarded *Bragg* with a constant stream of complaints. He asserted that the available facilities for transportation were inadequate, though other units sent that way in preceding weeks had moved much faster and encountered little difficulty. Having finally arrived outside Knoxville, he complained that he did not have nearly enough troops to accomplish his mission. In response to those complaints, *Bragg*, on November 22, audaciously elected to send him two more divisions – about 10,000 men – at a time when Grant already outnumbered him and would soon be receiving reinforcements. *Bragg* would have known that his chances of decisive success were slim if he simply waited for Grant to act when he was ready. Rather than face probable defeat that way, *Bragg* not unreasonably chose to gamble by reinforcing *Longstreet*. Maybe with the extra troops *Longstreet* could accomplish something that would change the strategic situation before Grant could be ready to attack.

As it turned out, the attack was even closer than *Bragg* guessed. The very next day, November 23, Grant ordered Thomas's Army of the Cumberland to advance and seize Confederate outposts around a small hill called Orchard Knob, several hundred yards in front of Missionary Ridge. *Bragg* now realized that he would have to receive whatever attacks Grant might be contemplating right here. He was at least able to recall the troops he sent to reinforce *Longstreet* and get more than half of them back before the main battle opened the next day with the fight on Lookout Mountain and on *Bragg's* other flank.

Bragg's army had never before fought a purely defensive battle, simply waiting to receive enemy attacks in its entrenchments. *Bragg* had always tried to take the initiative. Furthermore, though Confederate artillery had been emplaced on this ridgetop since late September, the Confederate infantry line had always occupied rifle pits along the base of the ridge. Realizing that he would be receiving an attack, *Bragg* on November 23 tried to avail himself of the height of the ridge to strengthen his defense and ordered that the main defensive line be drawn at the top of the ridge. Laying out a line on a ridge like this one was not nearly as simple as it might seem (as we shall see in subsequent stops), and *Bragg* was further handicapped in that endeavor by the absence of his chief engineer, Danville *Leadbetter*, whom he had dispatched to Knoxville to aid *Longstreet*. During the latter part of the twenty-third and all of the twenty-fourth, while other Confederates fought on Lookout Mountain, the troops here prepared their new defenses.

Further Reading   Sword, *Mountains Touched with Fire,* 186–94; Franks, "The Detachment of Longstreet Considered," 29–65.

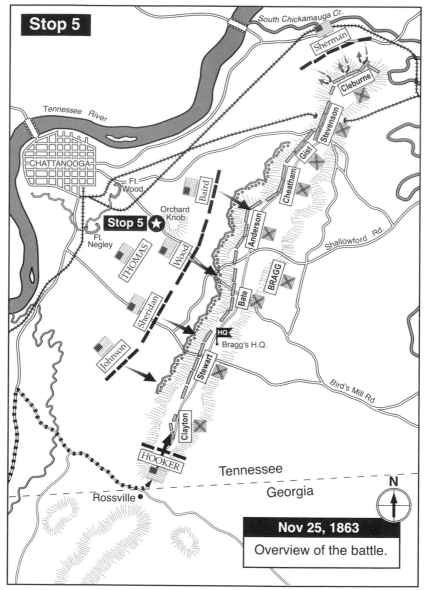

Stop 5

Tennessee River

CHATTANOOGA

South Chickamauga Cr.

Sherman

Cleburne

Stevenson

Gist

Cheatham

Baird

Ft. Wood

Orchard Knob

Stop 5 ★

Anderson

Shallowford Rd.

Ft. Negley

THOMAS

Wood

BRAGG

Bate

Sheridan

HQ
Bragg's H.Q.

Johnson

Stewart

Bird's Mill Rd

Clayton

HOOKER

Tennessee

Georgia

N

Rossville ●

Nov 25, 1863

Overview of the battle.

STOP 5   **Grant Watches the Battle Unfold**   November 25

Directions   *Turn right* and then *right again* out of the parking lot so that you are once again on CREST ROAD, driving in the same direction you were before the previous stop. *Drive* 1.4 miles to SHALLOWFORD ROAD. *En route* you will see a spectacular view of Chattanooga on your left shortly before reaching Shallowford Road. Don't stop now. Chattanooga optional excursion 1, Missionary Ridge, will provide an opportunity for you to take in this vista safely. *Turn left* on SHALLOWFORD ROAD. *Proceed*

0.6 mile to GLENMONT STREET. *Turn right. Proceed* 0.1 mile to IVY STREET. *Turn left. Continue* straight 0.6 mile to HAWTHORNE. *Turn right. Proceed* 1 block. Turn right on EAST 4TH STREET. Park on the right side of the street as soon as possible thereafter. Walk back to near the corner of EAST 4TH STREET and HAWTHORNE, where there is a gate and a paved pathway to the top of Orchard Knob. Walk to the top of the hill, to the Illinois Monument and nearby cannon. Face the direction the cannon are pointing.

Orientation   Missionary Ridge is more or less visible beyond the trees in front of you. In 1863 Orchard Knob lay well outside of Chattanooga.

What Happened   Orchard Knob was Grant's headquarters on November 25, from which he watched his battle plan produce victory in a way much different than he had planned.

Grant's plan was to use Sherman's Army of the Tennessee to crush *Bragg's* right (to your left) at the far end of Missionary Ridge.

Sherman encountered difficulty, however, and Grant decided to take further steps against the other portions of the Confederate line. Specifically, Hooker, proceeding from the position he had gained on Lookout Mountain the day before, was to get across Chattanooga Creek and onto Missionary Ridge at Rossville Gap (where you passed the Iowa Monument and turned onto South Crest Road), south of the Confederate positions, where he could roll up the Confederate left.

When Hooker was delayed by a missing bridge over Chattanooga Creek (the Confederates had burned the bridge after retreating across it the night before), and Grant watched from this position as Sherman's troops were driven off the northern end of the ridge, he decided it was time to modify his plan. His previous idea had been for the Army of the Cumberland to advance against the Confederate lines on and in front of Missionary Ridge only after one or both of the Confederate flanks had been crushed. Now, with both flank attacks stalled, Grant decided to try the Confederate center—Missionary Ridge directly in front of you. At about 3:30 P.M., he ordered Army of the Cumberland commander George H. Thomas to send his troops up the ridge. The result could have been an appalling slaughter of the advancing Federals. Instead, it was spectacular victory, as you'll see in detail in future stops.

Analysis   Critics have argued that Grant deserves little if any credit for the victory at Chattanooga since it was, they say, an accident that took place despite his plan rather than because of it. After all, they point out, Grant intended Sherman to make the dramatic breakthrough, gain the crest of the ridge, and roll up the Confederate line. In a word, they say Grant was just lucky.

Perhaps. Yet one is reminded of the famous German general and victor of the Franco-Prussian War, Helmut von Moltke, who said, "Luck is the residue of good planning" and "Good generals make their own luck." So it was with Grant. He pushed on *Bragg's* line in several places. It did not give way where he intended it to, but it did give way. Grant deserves credit for knowing that if he pushed in those places, the line had to give way somewhere. In fact, that was Grant's way of making war—constant pressure on all fronts until the enemy broke at some point. If Grant won by luck, it was "luck" he not only manufactured but also carried with him throughout the war.

Further Reading   Cozzens, *Shipwreck of Their Hopes*, 246–319; McDonough, *Chattanooga*, 161–219.

Note: As you make your way back to your car and reach East 4th Street again, walk eastward, away from the corner of Hawthorne Street and toward Missionary Ridge, until you have a clear view of the ridge. Look for the large open area just below the crest. It's the one near a large house with a castlelike left side (really a sort of turret). That is the location of the spectacular view that you glimpsed from the ridge as you drove here. It is also one of the first points at which Thomas's men reached the crest.

Bridging Lookout
Creek preparatory to
the assault by Hooker.
BLCW 3:699

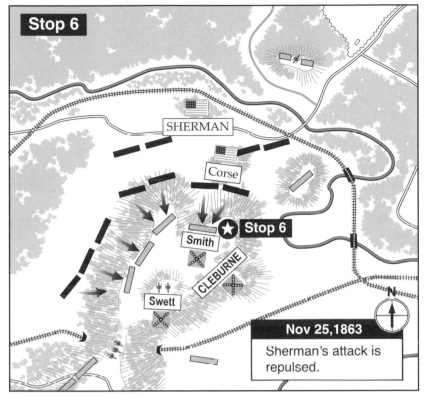

STOP 6

Sherman's Assault Falters November 25

Directions

Proceed to the corner of EAST 4TH STREET and ORCHARD KNOB AVENUE. *Turn right. Proceed* one block to IVY STREET. *Turn left. Proceed* 0.6 mile to GLENWOOD. *Turn right.* Go 0.1 mile to OAK STREET (which soon becomes SHALLOWFORD ROAD). *Turn left. Proceed* 0.6 mile to NORTH CREST ROAD. *Turn left.* Drive a little more than 2.4 miles to GREENWOOD ROAD. *Turn left. Proceed* about 0.1 mile to LIGHTFOOT MILL ROAD. *Turn right, then immediately turn left* on NORTH CREST ROAD. *Proceed* just over 0.2 mile and park in the parking lot at the end of the street. Walk up the paved walkway to the crest and then turn right and walk uphill along the crest to the monument and cannon of *Swett's* Mississippi Battery. As you walk you'll be covering the final yards of one of Sherman's attacks on the Confederate position, advancing as Sherman's troops advanced. Some of them got to within 20 yards of the guns ahead of you. Upon reaching the guns, turn around and face back the way you came.

Orientation

You are standing on Tunnel Hill, the northernmost high knob of Missionary Ridge and the position held by the Confederate troops of *Cleburne's* division on November 25. The railroad tunnel, from which the hill takes its name, is lo-cated a few hundred yards behind you. Sherman's men at-tacked up the hill toward where you are now standing.

What Happened

Grant intended the Federal victory to be won here, by his trusted lieutenant, Sherman, and his trusted soldiers of the Army of the Tennessee, the men who had taken Vicksburg under his command. They were as good as any soldiers in the war, but here they were asked to do the impossible. When Sherman's men took the lower lump of the ridge at the far end of the grassy area in front of you (about 400 yards north), he thought he had *Bragg* by the neck, sitting right on top of the ridge with him, right on his flank. It was not an unrea-sonable assumption, but it could not possibly take account of Pat *Cleburne* and the complicated nature of the ridge's topog-raphy. *Cleburne* cleverly used terrain to his advantage. Sher-man, attacking along the crest, was able to get into action only a fraction of the force under his command. They charged resolutely, took heavy casualties, and fought on bravely for hours on these slopes, but to no avail. The Confederate lines here remained unshakable.

Swett's Battery was a target of several of the Union attacks, including the first major Union assault at about 11:00 A.M. The midwesterners of Brig. Gen. John M. Corse's brigade scrambled resolutely up the hill toward this position. Infan-trymen of Brig. Gen. James A. *Smith's* Texas brigade opened fire at a range of 400 yards, and then *Swett's* Battery joined in with canister. Corse's men were driven back several times but came on again, as it seemed to one Texan, "like they were going to walk right over us." Some got to within 20 yards of the Confederates' log breastworks here, but the line could go no further. Corse was wounded and carried to the rear, and his surviving soldiers fell back to find what cover they could further down the slope and snipe at any Confederate who showed himself above the breastworks here. By this time, the badly exposed gunners of *Swett's* Battery had been so reduced that command had devolved on a corporal, as the senior sur-vivor, and volunteers from the infantry had to help man the guns.

Analysis

The Union failure here was a result of difficult terrain and an excellent Confederate defense. *Cleburne* used his troops and the terrain wisely, carefully positioning his forces to cover every possible approach and channel attackers into killing zones. He also reacted alertly to the developing battle situa-tion, shifting reserves to the points most threatened.

Sherman could employ only a fraction of his numerical

superiority (in fact a single brigade) along the crest of the ridge in front of you, and as you can see, the undulating nature of the ridge's crest gives defenders here an ideal height advantage over attackers coming toward you–so much for being on the ridge. When Sherman tried to deploy his additional troops to hit the other faces of the ridge (especially that to your left and left rear), he found that the rough, deeply ravined base of the ridge made it prohibitively difficult to march troops into position and impossible to coordinate attacks from different sectors seeking to converge on this hilltop.

By contrast, when the attacks did go up the slope, *Cleburne* had availed himself of the open view from here and the smooth nature of the summit to recognize the threat and move the needed reinforcements into position to defeat the assaults.

Further Reading   Sword, *Mountains Touched with Fire*, 240–47; McDonough, *Chattanooga*, 117–28.

Further Exploration   Contrary to legends that abounded at the time of the battle and since, the Confederates did not use the railroad tunnel to move troops through the ridge and thus outflank attackers on the west slope. They did, however, use the ravine, or fold in the slope, around the mouth of the tunnel to move troops down the west face and thus gain an important advantage in some of their local counterattacks. To view the west mouth of the tunnel, *drive back* the way you came on CREST AVENUE to LIGHTFOOT MILL ROAD. *Turn right* then immediately *turn right again* on CAMPBELL STREET (GREENWOOD ROAD). *Proceed* about 0.2 mile to GLASS STREET. *Turn left. Proceed* 3 blocks to AWTREY STREET. *Turn left*, then *go straight* (AWTREY turns left, but you continue straight on what is now called ARNO STREET). Just beyond the railroad overpass (0.1 mile from GLASS STREET) *turn left* onto STEPHENS STREET. *Proceed* about another 0.1 mile to a point where STEPHENS STREET and the railroad bed are level with each other. Park and walk 220 yards north (the same direction as you were driving a moment ago) to the tunnel.

To return to the main tour after viewing the tunnel, continue on STEPHENS STREET, which loops around and rejoins ARNO STREET near the railroad overpass. Reverse the above instructions until you come to CAMPBELL STREET (GREENWOOD ROAD). *Turn right. Proceed* about 0.3 mile to NORTH CREST ROAD. *Turn right. Proceed* about 1.9 miles to DeLong Reservation. Park in the parking area on the right.

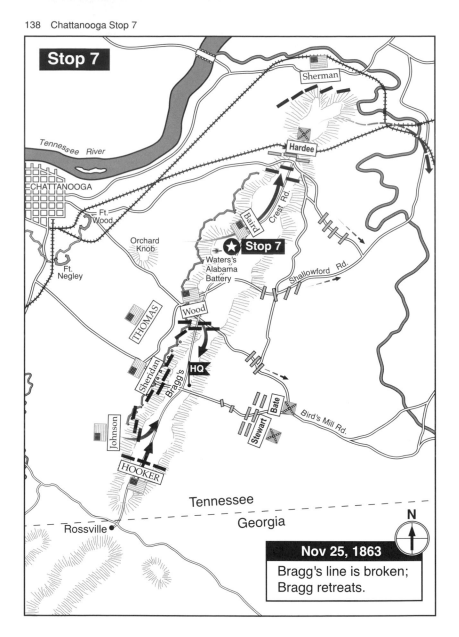

Nov 25, 1863

Bragg's line is broken;
Bragg retreats.

STOP 7 **The Storming of Missionary Ridge** November 25

Directions *Drive back* the way you came on DURAND AVENUE to LIGHTFOOT MILL ROAD. *Turn right. Proceed* not quite 0.2 mile to CAMPBELL STREET (GREENWOOD ROAD). *Turn left. Proceed* about 0.1 mile to NORTH CREST ROAD. *Turn right. Proceed* about 1.9 miles to De-Long Reservation. Park in the parking area on the right.

En route, as you drive along Crest Road, you are following a course just a few yards in front of the Confederate lines on Missionary Ridge. In fact, the Confederates would have done better to have placed their lines almost directly on the modern-day course of Crest Road. Instead, their lines were in most places several yards to your left, on the geographic crest or highest point of the ridge. That blocked their field of fire for significant parts of the slope. You will see monuments and plaques as you drive, but stopping to view them is a traffic hazard.

Walk to the far end of the small "reservation" and face in the same direction the cannons face.

Orientation   You are in a Confederate defensive position. The Federal troops charged up the ridge toward where you now stand.

What Happened   This is one of the few places where you can park, get out, and look over the terrain of the famous Missionary Ridge assault.

This position is also somewhat unusual as it is the highest and furthest outward jutting spur of the ridge in this area. It thus made an ideal position for the guns of *Waters's* Alabama Battery, who used it to good effect against the Federals farther to your left as they started up the ridge. Its drawback was its very steepness. The men of the 2nd Minnesota, leading Van Derveer's brigade, though taking heavy casualties, were able to creep up the nearly vertical slope where *Waters's* guns could not bear directly on them. They clambered over the log breastworks here and fought hand-to-hand with the gunners and the Alabama infantrymen of Brig. Gen. Zachariah *Deas's* brigade. "As my men sprang over the works," Van Derveer later wrote, "the enemy's cannoneers were caught in the act of loading and were bayoneted or driven off before they could fire their pieces." Five of the battery's six guns were captured, the Confederates managing to shove the other over the edge of the ridge to deny it to the victorious Federals, who also took large numbers of prisoners.

Analysis   This incident illustrates two of the factors that made the Union assault successful against all the established rules of Civil War combat.

1. The steep, rugged, uneven terrain of the ridge actually favored the attackers by affording many of them at least partial cover for at least some portion of the advance up the ridge. Even on the most exposed sections of ridge, the attackers could pause just under the crest to catch their breath and prepare for a coordinated final rush. Though Missionary Ridge looked daunting, a moderate rise with a smooth, open, gentle slope affording a full field of fire would have been far easier to defend.

2. Extreme determination and aggressiveness were exhib-

ited by the attacking Army of the Cumberland troops. They were anxious to redeem the blot on their record from Chickamauga and prove to Grant and the units from the other two Federal armies represented in Chattanooga that they could fight well.

Vignette

This last factor is illustrated by the experience of Sergeant Axel Reed of the 2nd Minnesota. In the close-in fighting over the guns of *Waters's* Alabama Battery (on this very ground), Reed took a bullet in the right arm, shattering the bone just below the elbow. He managed to get a crude tourniquet on it and avoid bleeding to death. Then came the ordeal of the field hospital. Civil War medicine knew only one treatment for the sort of wound caused when a soft lead .58 caliber slug smashed into human bone. Surgeons plied the bone saw freely, and amputations were so common that field hospitals during major battles were marked by piles of severed arms and legs. After Reed's right arm was removed, he remarked, "I had rather have that, that way, than to have been whipped by the rebels up there."

Further Reading

Cozzens, *Shipwreck of Their Hopes*, 280, 327–29; McDonough, *Chattanooga*, 197–98.

General Hooker and staff on the hill north of Lookout Creek, from which he directed the battle. From a photograph. BLCW 3:722

Optional Excursions

OPTIONAL EXCURSION 1   Missionary Ridge Walking Tour

If you can possibly spare the time and handle about two miles of easy walking, you should definitely plan to take advantage of this opportunity to view Missionary Ridge. As you've gathered by now, Crest Road is no place for parking or even driving slow and taking in the sights. Parking near most of the desirable locations further along the ridge would be illegal and dangerous and is definitely not recommended, but you can see it all–better–with this brief walking tour.

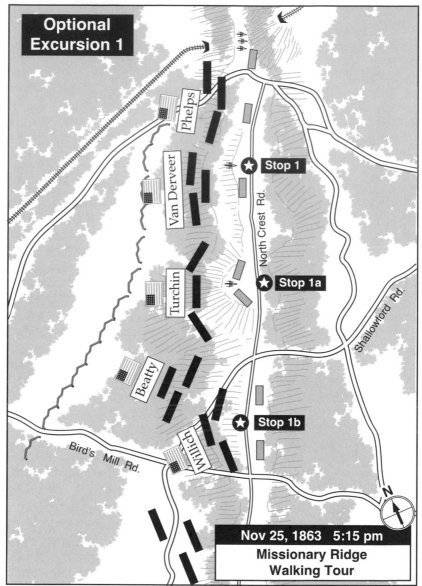

Within the map:

Optional Excursion 1

Phelps

Van Derveer

Turchin

Beatty

North Crest Rd.

Shallowford Rd.

⭐ Stop 1

⭐ Stop 1a

⭐ Stop 1b

Willich

Bird's Mill Rd.

N

Nov 25, 1863   5:15 pm
Missionary Ridge
Walking Tour

Excursion Stop 1a   Turchin Takes a Battery   November 25

Directions

Leaving your car at the DeLong Reservation, continue walking in the direction you were last driving (south), using the sidewalk across the street. About 600 yards from the DeLong Reservation, you will come to the Turchin Reservation. Stand anywhere in this postage-stamp-sized park and face the same direction the cannons face.

Orientation

You are standing on another of those forward projections of the crest. Here, as at the DeLong Reservation, the Confederates made use of the spur as an emplacement for artillery and ran their line forward to this point rather than keeping it on the very highest part of the ridge, which would be behind you. The slope just in front of this point is extremely steep, providing the attackers with shelter on their approach and especially as they gathered themselves for the final rush. Since the battle, however, a stone retaining wall has been built on the downhill side of the reservation, altering the terrain.

What Happened

Here troops of Brig. Gen. John Turchin's brigade stormed the crest, the first to do so in this sector, though others probably got to the top before them further south.

Turchin's men were a bit behind their neighboring units, Van Derveer on their left (your right) and Beatty on their right, in taking the rifle pits at the base of the ridge, but Turchin, a colorful Russian immigrant who had once been an officer in the czar's army, was much quicker in ordering his troops on up the ridge. They suffered a severe enfilading fire from *Waters's* Battery on the spur that is now DeLong Reservation. Three of Turchin's regiments nevertheless pressed on and captured this point, taking the two guns of *Dent's* Alabama Battery that had been stationed here. Turchin's other regiments passed to either side, and one veered north to help Van Derveer's men take *Waters's* Battery.

Despite the presence of a tablet here representing Samuel Beatty's brigade, that unit in fact charged on Turchin's left and bore further south as it advanced, reaching the top of the ridge in the vicinity of the Shallowford Road somewhat after Turchin carried the crest here. Beatty's brigade then moved northward along the crest, rolling up the Confederate defenders between here and the Shallowford Road and, at least according to Turchin, laying claim to cannon that had actually been taken from the Rebels by Turchin's men. Turchin's brigade meanwhile turned north and helped Van Derveer's troops drive the Confederates well north of the present-day site of DeLong Reservation.

Excursion Stop 1b First Breakthrough November 25

Directions

Continue walking along the sidewalk another 700 yards until you come to the spectacular view that you noted while driving past this spot, a high knoll with an absence of trees and houses that allows a clear view of Chattanooga. *En route* you will pass a monument commemorating the 8th Kansas as well as a tablet representing August Willich's brigade, of which the 8th was a part. In fact, Willich's troops reached the crest in this area and as far north as the Shallowford Road. From there some of them, including the 8th Kansas, turned northward along the crest to exploit the breakthrough, and that explains the presence of their monuments north of the Shallowford Road.

Orientation

This vista allows you to realize the amphitheater-like form of the Chattanooga area and the unusually dramatic nature of a battle fought in it and on the surrounding hills. It also gives you a clear view, straight ahead, of Orchard Knob (Chattanooga stop 4), from which Grant watched the battle unfold. It is the small, tree-covered knoll at the point where the street directly in front of you dead-ends. The part of Missionary Ridge where you now stand was held by another section of *Dent's* Alabama Battery, supported by the infantry of Col. W. F. *Tucker's* Mississippi brigade.

What Happened

This panoramic view gives you the opportunity to try to visualize the scene Confederate soldiers, standing where you now do, witnessed as the Union assault began. Thomas's 23,000 men were ranged in parade-ground order across the plain below you, forming up just in front of Orchard Knob and extending a considerable distance to either side. "Such a sight I never saw either before or after," wrote Confederate general Arthur *Manigault*, "and I trust . . . never to see again." Rarely on the battlefields of the Civil War were troops able to see such a large portion of their own or the enemy's army, and the sight may have unnerved the Rebel defenders here. "I noticed some nervousness among my men as they beheld this grand military spectacle," recalled *Manigault*. At the same time, the Confederates on the ridge could have seen at most a few hundred of their own men, in line on either side of them along the crest. Comparing the view in front of you to that on either side will help you understand why.

This was the first point at which Union troops reached the crest of the ridge. The attackers here belonged to Willich's brigade, with the men of Hazen's brigade close behind just to your left. Once they closed in on this position, the fight was over quickly. The Confederates fled, leaving their cannon behind.

Analysis

Besides those mentioned at previous stops, several factors contributed to Confederate defeat.

1. The faulty deployment of the Confederate forces, with half the troops in the rifle pits at the bottom of the ridge and

half in line here, robbed either line of maximum strength and created a situation in which the fleeing soldiers from the bottom of the ridge blocked the field of fire of those at the top.

2. The poor location of the ridgetop line at the geographical crest (highest point) rather than the military crest of the ridge created large areas on the forward slope where attacking Federals could shelter from Confederate fire.

3. The constant infighting of the generals and the backbiting and criticism against *Bragg* had apparently filtered down through the ranks by this time and created an atmosphere of distrust that had made the troops susceptible to demoralization. Soldiers who believe their lives will be sacrificed to no purpose by an incompetent commander are not likely to be resolute in battle.

Before returning to your vehicle, walk on another 400 yards to Bird's Mill Road. By turning right and walking a short distance down Bird's Mill Road, you can gain a better appreciation of the terrain on the forward slope of Missionary Ridge.

Retracing your steps to DeLong Reservation concludes your tour of the Chattanooga battlefields.

Further Reading   McDonough, *Chattanooga*, 174–87; Sword, *Mountains Touched with Fire*, 266–95.

Looking for a Friend. BLCW 4:1

After Chattanooga

The collapse of the Confederate defenses atop Missionary Ridge was almost complete. Thomas's troops overran the center of *Bragg's* line, and Hooker's, having marched down from Lookout Mountain, across Chattanooga Creek on an improvised bridge, and up Missionary Ridge at Rossville Gap (where you turned left onto South Crest Road near the tall column of the Iowa Monument), beyond the Confederate left, crushed that end of the Army of Tennessee. Only at the north end of Missionary Ridge, the Confederate right, where *Cleburne* had held off Sherman all day at Tunnel Hill, did Confederate forces maintain their cohesion. *Cleburne*, using his own division and two others that *Bragg* had sent earlier in the day to his support, turned to face the threat of Union troops moving up the ridge from the south. His unbroken front— along with Federal exhaustion and the gathering darkness— stopped the Union advance. Then *Cleburne* and his force slowly withdrew, covering the disorderly retreat of the rest of the army. Most of the Federal troops and their commanders had had enough fighting for one day. An exception was the hard-driving Union division commander Philip Sheridan, who pressed on into the darkness and sparred with *Cleburne's* rear guard all the way to Chickamauga Creek (well downstream from the old battleground).

The Confederate army was routed, but it had escaped to fight again. This was largely because its line of retreat–the bridges over Chickamauga Creek and the railroad running back toward Atlanta–lay behind the Confederate right. That was the sector Grant had most wanted to smash, but *Cleburne's* skill and tenacity–and the fighting qualities of his men–had prevented that. Thus when the rest of the army broke, it had an open line of retreat, and *Cleburne's* force was well positioned to fend off Union pursuit.

Grant was already under considerable pressure from Washington to do something to assist Burnside, then facing a quasi-siege by *Longstreet's* force at Knoxville. For this reason Grant had intended to dispatch a major detachment to Knoxville as soon as *Bragg* was driven away from Chattanooga. Seeing the completeness of the Confederate rout, however, Grant changed his mind and decided to try a brief pursuit in hopes of seriously damaging or even destroying the beaten Rebel army.

Throughout the day after the battle, Thursday, November 26, his troops pressed after the retreating Confederates. On the twenty-seventh, Hooker's command came upon *Cleburne*, still commanding *Bragg's* rear guard and now positioned in a mountain pass at Ringgold Gap (just east of the present-day town of Ringgold, Georgia; six miles southeast of Chattanooga on U.S. 41). Though his artillery had not come up yet, Hooker correctly judged that his only chance to catch *Bragg's* retiring supply wagon train was to push on through the gap at once, keeping up the momentum of the pursuit. Skillfully handling his troops and taking full advantage of favorable terrain, *Cleburne* administered a sharp check to Hooker's pursuit. Then, having gained the time needed for the supply wagons to make good their escape, he retired from the gap and followed them south. Grant realized that continued pursuit offered no further prospect of quick gains. Most of his available force, the Army of the Cumberland, was all but immobile because of the widespread death and emaciation of draft animals during the Chattanooga siege, and he needed to get a contingent started for Burnside at once.

Giving up the chase, then, Grant sent Sherman to relieve Knoxville. *Longstreet* retired into extreme northeastern Tennessee and by the next spring had returned to *Lee* in Virginia. Thereafter no one, including *Longstreet*, ever again advocated his holding an independent command. *Bragg*, too, had come to the end of his career as an army commander. After Chattanooga he again asked to be relieved, and this time *Davis* lost no time in doing so, appointing William J. *Hardee* as temporary commander and subsequently General Joseph E. *Johnston* to hold the post on a regular basis. *Johnston's* army spent the winter near Dalton, Georgia, fortifying an eminence called Rocky-face Ridge and preparing to meet the Union advance that was bound to come in the spring (I-75 passes through a gap in Rocky-face near Dalton about 20 miles south of Chattanooga).

By that time Grant had been promoted to commanding general of all Union forces and was preparing a coordinated nationwide offensive that would eventually crush the life out of the Confederacy. While Grant himself would personally supervise the action in Virginia, the second most important part of his plan would be launched from Chattanooga. Sherman, leading the Army of the Tennessee, the Army of the Cumberland, and the Army of the Ohio (Burnside's old command) would advance southeastward toward Atlanta and, beyond it, to the sea.

Appendix A: Chickamauga Orders of Battle

Union Forces

ARMY OF THE CUMBERLAND (Rosecrans)

XIV Army Corps (Thomas)

Abbreviations:

BDE: Brigade

BN: Battalion

C.S.: Confederate States

M.R.: Mounted Rifles, Dismounted

S.S.: Sharpshooters

A notation such as 2/5 indicates the second battalion of the fifth regiment.

1st Division (Baird)

1ST BDE (Scribner)	2ND BDE (Starkweather)	3RD BDE (J. King)
38th IN	24th IL	1/15th U.S.
2nd OH	79th PA	1/16th U.S.
33rd OH	1st WI	1/18th U.S.
94th OH	21st WI	2/18th U.S.
10th WI		1/19th U.S.

ARTILLERY: 4th IN Battery (Flansburg); Battery A, 1st MI (Van Pelt); Battery H, 5th U.S. (Burnham)

2nd Division (Negley)

1ST BDE (J. Beatty)	2ND BDE (Stanley)	3RD BDE (Sirwell)
104th IL	19th IL	37th IN
42nd IN	11th MI	21st OH
88th IN	18th OH	74th OH
15th KY		78th PA

ARTILLERY: Bridges's (IL) Battery; Battery G, 1st OH (Marshall); Battery M, 1st OH (Schultz)

3rd Division (Brannan)

1ST BDE (Connell)	2ND BDE (Croxton)	3RD BDE (Van Derveer)
82nd IN	10th IN	87th IN
17th OH	74th IN	2nd MN
31st OH	4th KY	9th OH
38th OH	10th KY	35th OH
	14th OH	

ARTILLERY: Battery D, 1st MI (Church); Battery C, 1st OH (Gary); Battery I, 4th U.S. (Smith)

4th Division (Reynolds)

1ST BDE (Wilder)	2ND BDE (E. King)	3RD BDE (Turchin)
92nd IL	68th IN	18th KY
98th IL	75th IN	11th OH
123rd IL	101st IN	36th OH
17th IN	105th OH	92nd OH
72nd IN		

ARTILLERY: 18th IN Battery (Lilly); 19th IN Battery (Harris); 21st IN Battery (Andrew)

Left: General Ulysses S. Grant in a photograph taken after the war. BLCW 4:105

XX Army Corps (McCook)

1st Division (Davis)

	2ND BDE (Carlin)	3RD BDE (Heg)
	21st IL	25th IL
	38th IL	35th IL
	81st IN	8th KS
	101st OH	15th WI

ARTILLERY: 5th WI Battery (Gardner); 2nd MN Battery (Woodbury); 8th WI Battery (McLean)

2nd Division (R. Johnson)

1ST BDE (Willich)	2ND BDE (Dodge)	3RD BDE (Baldwin)
89th IL	79th IL	6th IN
32nd IN	29th IN	5th KY
39th IN	30th IN	1st OH
15th OH	77th PA	
49th OH		

ARTILLERY: Battery A, 1st OH (Goodspeed); 5th IN Battery (Simonson)

3rd Division (Sheridan)

1ST BDE (Lytle)	2ND BDE (Laiboldt)	3RD BDE (Bradley)
36th IL	44th IL	22nd IL
88th IL	73rd IL	27th IL
21st MI	2nd MO	42nd IL
24th WI	15th MO	51st IL

ARTILLERY: 11th IN Battery, (Sutermeister); Battery G, 1st MO (Schueler); Battery C, 1st IL (Prescott)

XXI Army Corps (Crittenden)

1st Division (Wood)

1ST BDE (Buell)	2ND BDE (Wagner)	3RD BDE (Harker)
100th IL	15th IN	3rd KY
58th IN	40th IN	64th OH
13th MI	57th IN	65th OH
26th OH	97th OH	125th OH

ARTILLERY: 8th IN Battery (Estep); 10th IN Battery (Naylor); 6th OH Battery (Bradley)

2nd Division (Palmer)

1ST BDE (Cruft)	2ND BDE (Hazen)	3RD BDE (Grose)
31st IN	9th IN	84th IL
1st KY	6th KY	36th IN
2nd KY	41st OH	23rd KY
90th OH	124th OH	6th OH
		24th OH

ARTILLERY: Battery B, 1st OH (Baldwin); Battery F, 1st OH (Cockerill); Battery H, 4th U.S.; Battery M, 4th U.S.

3rd Division (Van Cleve)

1ST BDE (S. Beatty)	2ND BDE (Dick)	3RD BDE (Barnes)
79th IN	44th IN	35th IN
9th KY	86th IN	8th KY
17th KY	13th OH	21st KY
19th OH	59th OH	51st OH
		99th OH

ARTILLERY: 7th IN Battery (Swallow); 26th PA Battery (Stevens); 3rd WI Battery (Livingston)

Reserve Corps (Granger)

1st Division (Steedman)

1ST BDE (Whitaker)	2ND BDE (Mitchell)
96th IL	78th IL
115th IL	98th OH
84th IN	113th OH
22nd MI	121st OH
40th OH	1st IL
89th OH	

ARTILLERY: 18th OH Battery (Aleshire)

Cavalry Corps (Mitchell)

1st Division (E. McCook)

1ST BDE (Campbell)	2ND BDE (Ray)	3RD BDE (Watkins)
2nd MI	2nd IN	4th KY
9th PA	4th IN	5th KY
1st TN	2nd TN	6th KY
	1st WI	

ARTILLERY: Battery D, 1st OH (Newell)

2nd Division (Crook)

1ST BDE (Minty)	2ND BDE (Long)
3rd IN Bn.	2nd KY
4th MI	1st OH
7th PA	3rd OH
4th U.S.	4th OH

ARTILLERY: Chicago Board of Trade Battery (Stokes)

Confederate Forces   ARMY OF TENNESSEE (Bragg)

Right Wing (Polk)

Cheatham's Division

JACKSON'S BDE	SMITH'S BDE	MANEY'S BDE	WRIGHT'S BDE	STRAHL'S BDE
2/1st GA	11th TN	1st & 27th TN	8th TN	4th & 5th TN
5th GA	12th & 47th TN	4th TN	16th TN	19th TN
2nd GA Bn. S.S.	13th & 154th TN	6th & 9th TN	28th TN	24th TN
5th MS	29th TN	24th TN Bn. S.S.	38th TN	31st TN
8th MS	Dawson's Bn. S.S.	51st & 52nd TN	33rd TN	

ARTILLERY: Carnes's TN Battery; Scogin's GA Battery; Scott's TN Battery (Marsh); Smith's MS Battery (Turner); Stanford's MS Battery

Hill's Corps

Cleburne's Division

WOOD'S BDE	POLK'S BDE	DESHLER'S BDE
16th AL	1st AR	9th & 24th AR
33rd AL	3rd & 5th C.S.	6th, 10th & 15th TX
45th AL	2nd TN	17th, 18th, 24th, & 25th TX
18th AL Bn.	35th TN	
32nd & 45th MS	48th TN	
15th MS Bn. S.S.		

ARTILLERY: Calvert's AR Battery (Key); Douglas's TX Battery; Semple's AL Battery

Breckinridge's Division

HELM'S BDE	ADAMS'S BDE	STOVALL'S BDE
41st AL	32nd AL	1st & 3rd FL
2nd KY	13th & 20th LA	4th FL
4th KY	16th & 25th LA	47th GA
6th KY	19th LA	60th NC
9th KY	14th LA Bn.	

ARTILLERY: Cobb's KY Battery; Graves's KY Battery (Spencer); Mebane's TN Battery; Slocomb's LA Battery

Reserve Corps (Walker)

Walker's Division (Gist)

GIST'S BDE (Colquitt)	ECTOR'S BDE	WILSON'S BDE
46th GA	Stone's AL Bn. S.S.	25th GA
8th GA Bn.	Pound's MS Bn. S.S.	29th GA
16th SC	29th NC	30th GA
24th SC	9th TX	1st GA Bn. S.S.
	10th TX	4th LA Bn.
	14th TX	
	32nd TX	

ARTILLERY: Ferguson's SC Battery (Beauregard); Howell's GA Battery

Liddell's Division

LIDDELL'S BDE (Govan)	WALTHALL'S BDE
2nd & 15th AR	24th MS
5th & 13th AR	27th MS
6th & 7th AR	29th MS
1st LA	30th MS
	34th MS

ARTILLERY: Fowler's AL Battery; Warren (MS) Light Artillery (Shannon)

Left Wing (Longstreet)

Hindman's Division

ANDERSON'S BDE	DEAS'S BDE	MANIGAULT'S BDE
7th MS	19th AL	24th AL
9th MS	22nd AL	28th AL
10th MS	25th AL	34th AL
41st MS	39th AL	10th & 19th SC
44th MS	50th AL	
9th MS Bn. S.S.	17th AL	

ARTILLERY: Garrity's AL Battery; Dent's AL Battery; Waters's AL Battery (Watkins)

Buckner's Corps

Stewart's Division

BATE'S BDE	BROWN'S BDE	CLAYTON'S BDE
58th AL	18th TN	18th AL
37th GA	26th TN	26th AL
4th GA Bn. S.S.	32nd TN	38th AL
15th & 37th TN	45th TN	
20th TN	23rd TN Bn.	

ARTILLERY: 1st AR Battery (Humphreys); Dawson's GA Battery (Anderson); Eufaula (AL) Artillery; Co. E, 9th GA Artillery Bn. (Everrett)

Preston's Division

GRACIE'S BDE	TRIGG'S BDE	3RD BDE (Kelly)
43rd AL	1st FL	65th GA
1st AL Bn.	6th FL	5th KY
2nd AL Bn.	7th FL	58th NC
3rd AL Bn.	54th VA	63rd VA
4th AL Bn.		
63rd TN		

ARTILLERY: Jeffress's VA Battery; Peeples's GA Battery; Wolihin's GA Battery

Johnson's Division

GREGG'S BDE	MCNAIR'S BDE	FULTON'S BDE
3rd TN	1st AR M.R.	17th TN
10th TN	2nd AR M.R.	23rd TN
41st TN	25th AR	25th TN
50th TN	4th & 31st AR & 4th AR Bn.	44th TN
1st TN Bn.	39th NC	
7th TX		

ARTILLERY: Bledsoe's (MO) Battery; Culpeper's (SC) Battery

Longstreet's Corps (Hood)

McLaw's Division (Kershaw)

KERSHAW'S BDE	HUMPHREYS'S BDE
2nd SC	13th MS
3rd SC	17th MS
7th SC	18th MS
8th SC	21st MS
15th SC	
3rd SC Bn.	

Hood's Division (Law)

LAW'S BDE (Sheffield)	ROBERTSON'S BDE	BENNING'S BDE
4th AL	3rd AR	2nd GA
15th AL	1st TX	15th GA
44th AL	4th TX	17th GA
47th AL	5th TX	20th GA
48th AL		

Reserve Artillery (Robertson)

Barret's MO Battery; Le Gardeur's LA Battery; Havis's GA Battery; Lumsden's AL Battery; Massenburg's GA Battery

Cavalry (Wheeler)

Wharton's Division

1ST BDE (Crews)	2ND BDE (Harrison)
Malone's AL Regt.	3rd C.S.
2nd GA	3rd KY
3rd GA	4th TN
4th GA	8th TX
	11th TX

ARTILLERY: White's TN Battery

Martin's Division

1ST BDE (Morgan)	2ND BDE (Russell)
1st AL	4th AL
3rd AL	1st C.S.
51st AL	
8th C.S.	

ARTILLERY: Wiggins's AR Battery (Bryant)

Forrest's Corps

Armstrong's Division

ARMSTRONG'S BDE (J. T. Wheeler)	FORREST'S BDE (Dibrell)
3rd AR	4th TN
2nd KY	8th TN
6th TN	9th TN
18th TN	10th TN
	11th TN
	Shaw's & Hamilton's Bns. & Allison's Squadron

ARTILLERY: Huggins's TN Battery; Morton's TN Battery

Pegram's Division

DAVIDSON'S BDE	SCOTT'S BDE
1st GA	10th C.S.
6th GA	1st LA
6th NC	2nd TN
Rucker's Legion	5th TN

ARTILLERY: Huwald's TN Battery; Robinson's LA Battery

Appendix B: Chattanooga Orders of Battle

Union Forces (Grant)

ARMY OF THE CUMBERLAND (Thomas)

IV Army Corps (Granger)

1st Division (Cruft)

Abbreviations:

BDE: Brigade

BN: Battalion

C.S.: Confederate States

M.R.: Mounted Rifles, Dismounted

S.S.: Sharpshooters

A notation such as 2/5 indicates the second battalion of the fifth regiment.

2ND BDE (Whitaker)	3RD BDE (Grose)
96th IL	59th IL
35th IN	75th IL
8th KY	84th IL
40th OH	9th IN
51st OH	36th IN
99th OH	24th OH

2nd Division (Sheridan)

1ST BDE (F. Sherman)	2ND BDE (Wagner)	3RD BDE (Harker)
36th IL	100th IL	22nd IL
44th IL	15th IN	27th IL
73rd IL	40th IN	42nd IL
74th IL	57th IN	51st IL
88th IL	58th IN	79th IL
22nd IN	26th OH	3rd KY
2nd MO	97th OH	64th OH
15th MO		65th OH
24th WI		125th OH

ARTILLERY: Battery M, 1st IL (Spencer); 10th IN Battery (Naylor); Battery G, 1st MO (Schueler); Battery I, 1st OH (Dilger); Battery G, 4th U.S. (Merkle); Battery H, 5th U.S. (Guenther)

3rd Division (Wood)

1ST BDE (Willich)	2ND BDE (Hazen)	3RD BDE (S. Beatty)
25th IL	6th IN	79th IN
35th IL	5th KY	86th IN
89th IL	6th KY	9th KY
32nd IN	23rd KY	17th KY
68th IN	1st OH	13th OH
8th KS	6th OH	19th OH
15th OH	41st OH	59th OH
49th OH	93rd OH	
15th WI	124th OH	

ARTILLERY: Bridges's (IL) Battery; 6th OH Battery (Ayres); 20th OH Battery (Grosskopff); Battery B, PA Light Artillery (McDowell)

XI Army Corps (Howard)

2nd Division (von Steinwehr)

1ST BDE (Buschbeck)	2ND BDE (Smith)
33rd NJ	33rd MA
134th NY	136th NY
154th NY	55th OH
27th PA	73rd OH
73rd PA	

3rd Division (Schurz)

1ST BDE (Tyndale)	2ND BDE (Krzyzanowski)	3RD BDE (Hecker)
101st IL	58th NY	80th IL
45th NY	119th NY	82nd IL
143rd NY	141st NY	68th NY
61st OH	26th WI	75th PA
82nd OH		

ARTILLERY: Battery I, 1st NY; 13th NY Battery (Wheeler); Battery K, 1st OH (Sahm)

XII Army Corps[1]

2nd Division (Geary)

1ST BDE (Candy)	2ND BDE (Cobham)	3RD BDE (Ireland)
5th OH	29th PA	60th NY
7th OH	109th PA	78th NY
29th OH	111th PA	102nd NY
66th OH		137th NY
28th PA		149th NY
147th PA		

ARTILLERY: Battery E, PA Light (McGill); Battery K, 5th U.S. (Bainbridge)

1. The First Division engaged in guarding the Nashville and Chattanooga Railroad from Wartrace Bridge, Tennessee, to Bridgeport, Alabama. Maj. Gen. H. W. Slocum, the corps commander, had his headquarters at Tullahoma, Tennessee.

XIV Army Corps (Palmer)

1st Division (R. Johnson)

1ST BDE (Carlin)	2ND BDE (Moore)	3RD BDE (Starkweather)
104th IL	19th IL	24th IL
38th IN	11th MI	37th IN
42nd IN	69th OH	21st OH
88th IN	1/15th U.S.	74th OH
2nd OH	2/15th U.S.	78th PA
33rd OH	1/16th U.S.	79th PA
94th OH	2/18th U.S.	1st WI
10th WI	1/19th U.S.	21st WI

ARTILLERY: Battery C, 1st IL (Prescott); Battery A, 1st MI (Hale)

2nd Division (Davis)

1ST BDE (Morgan)	2ND BDE (J. Beatty)	3RD BDE (D. McCook)
10th IL	34th IL	85th IL
16th IL	78th IL	86th IL
60th IL	3rd OH	110th IL
21st KY	98th OH	125th IL
10th MI	108th OH	52nd IL
	113th OH	
	121st OH	

ARTILLERY: Battery I, 2nd IL (Plant); 2nd MN Battery (Dawley); 5th WI Battery (Gardner)

3rd Division (Baird)

1ST BDE (Turchin)	2ND BDE (Van Derveer)	3RD BDE (Phelps)
82nd IN	75th IN	10th IN
11th OH	87th IN	74th IN
17th OH	101st IN	4th KY
31st OH	2nd MN	10th KY
36th OH	9th OH	14th OH
89th OH	35th OH	38th OH
92nd OH	105th OH	

ARTILLERY: 7th IN Battery (Morgan); 19th IN Battery (Lackey); Battery I, 4th U.S. (Smith)

Artillery Reserve (Brannan)

1st Division (Barnett)

1ST BDE (Cotter)	2ND BDE
Battery B, 1st OH (Baldwin)	Battery G, 1st OH (Marshall)
Battery C, 1st OH (Gary)	Battery M, 1st OH (Schultz)
Battery E, 1st OH (Ransom)	18th OH Battery (McCafferty)
Battery F, 1st OH (Cockerill)	

2nd Division

1ST BDE (Church)	2ND BDE (Sutermeister)
Battery D, 1st MI (Church)	4th IN Battery (Willits)
Battery A, 1st TN (Beach)	8th IN Battery (Estep)
3rd WI Battery (Hubbard)	11th IN Battery (Sutermeister)
8th WI Battery (German)	21st IN Battery (Chess)
10th WI Battery (Beebee)	Company C, 1st WI Heavy (Davies)

Cavalry

2ND BDE
(Long)

98th IL (mounted infantry)	17th IN (mounted infantry)
2nd KY	4th MI
1st OH	4th OH Bn.
3rd OH	10th OH

ARMY OF THE TENNESSEE (W. T. Sherman)

XV Army Corps (Blair)

1st Division (Osterhaus)

1ST BDE (Woods)	2ND BDE (Williamson)
13th IL	4th IA
3rd MO	9th IA
12th MO	25th IA
17th MO	26th IA
27th MO	30th IA
29th MO	31st IA
31st MO	
32nd MO	
76th OH	

ARTILLERY: 1st IA Battery (Williams); Battery F, 2nd MO (Landgraeber); 4th OH Battery (Froehlich)

2nd Division (G. A. Smith)

1ST BDE (G. A. Smith)	2ND BDE (Lightburn)
55th IL	83rd IN
116th IL	30th OH
27th IL	37th OH
6th MO	47th OH
8th MO	54th OH
57th OH	4th WV
1/13th U.S.	

ARTILLERY: Battery A, 1st IL (Wood); Battery B, 1st IL (Rumsey); Battery H, 1st IL (De Gress)

4th Division (Ewing)

1ST BDE (Loomis)	2ND BDE (Corse)	3RD BDE (Cockerill)
26th IL	40th IL	48th IL
90th IL	103rd IL	97th IN
12th IN	6th IA	99th IN
100th IN	46th OH	53rd OH
		70th OH

ARTILLERY: Battery F, 1st IL (Cheney); Battery I, 1st IL (Burton); Battery D, 1st MO (Callender)

XVII Army Corps

2nd Division (J. E. Smith)

1ST BDE (Alexander)	2ND BDE (Raum)	3RD BDE (Matthies)
63rd IL	56th IL	93rd IL
48th IN	17th IA	5th IA
59th IN	10th MO	10th IA
4th MN	24th MO	26th MO
18th WI	80th OH	

ARTILLERY: Cogswell's IL Battery; 6th WI Battery (Clark); 12th WI Battery (Zickerick)

Confederate Forces

ARMY OF TENNESSEE (Bragg)

Hardee's Army Corps

Cheatham's Division

JACKSON'S BDE	WALTHALL'S BDE	WRIGHT'S BDE
1st GA	24th & 27th MS	8th TN
5th GA	29th & 30th MS	16th TN
47th GA	34th MS	28th TN
65th GA		38th TN
2nd GA Bn. S.S.		51st & 52nd TN
5th MS		Murray's TN Bn.
8th MS		
37th AL		
40th AL		
42nd AL		

ARTILLERY: AL Battery (Fowler); FL Battery (McCants); GA Battery (Scogin); MS Battery (Turner)

Hindman's Division (Anderson)

ANDERSON'S BDE (Tucker)	MANIGAULT'S BDE	DEAS'S BDE	VAUGHAN'S BDE
7th MS	24th AL	19th AL	11th TN
9th MS	28th AL	22nd AL	12th & 47th TN
10th MS	34th AL	25th AL	13th & 154th TN
41st MS	10th & 19th SC	39th AL	
44th MS		50th AL	
9th MS Bn. S.S.		17th AL Bn. S.S.	

ARTILLERY: AL Battery (Dent); AL Battery (Garrity); TN Battery (Doscher); Waters's AL Battery (Hamilton)

Buckner's Division

REYNOLDS'S BDE

58th NC

60th NC

54th VA

63rd VA

ARTILLERY: Darden's MS Battery (Bullen); VA Battery (Jeffress); AL Battery (Kolb)

Walker's Division

MANEY'S BDE	GIST'S BDE	WILSON'S BDE
1st & 27th TN	46th GA	25th GA
4th TN	8th GA Bn.	29th GA
6th & 9th TN	16th SC	30th GA
41st TN	24th SC	26th GA Bn.
50th TN		1st GA Bn. S.S.
24th TN Bn. S.S.		

ARTILLERY: Martin's MO Battery; Bledsoe's SC Battery; Ferguson's GA Battery (Howell)

Breckinridge's Army Corps

Cleburne's Division

LIDDELL'S BDE	SMITH'S BDE	POLK'S BDE	LOWREY'S BDE
2nd & 15th AR	6th, 10th, & 15th TX	1st AR	16th AL
5th & 13th AR	7th TX	3rd & 5th C.S.	33rd AL
6th & 7th AR	17th, 18th, 24th, & 25th TX	2nd TN	45th AL
8th AR		35th & 48th TN	32nd & 45th MS
19th & 24th AR			15th MS Bn. S.S.

Stewart's Division

ADAM'S BDE	STRAHL'S BDE	CLAYTON'S BDE	STOVALL'S BDE
13th & 20th LA	4th & 5th TN	18th AL	40th GA
16th & 25th LA	19th TN	32nd AL	41st GA
19th LA	24th TN	36th AL	42nd GA
4th LA Bn.	31st TN	38th AL	43rd GA
14th LA Bn. S.S.	33rd TN	58th AL	52nd GA

ARTILLERY: Dawson's GA Battery (Anderson); Humphreys's AR Battery (Rivers); AL Battery (Oliver); MS Battery (Stanford)

Breckinridge's Division (Bate)

LEWIS'S BDE	BATE'S BDE (Tyler)	FL BDE (Finley)
2nd KY	37th GA	1st & 3rd FL
4th KY	4th GA Bn. S.S.	4th FL
5th KY	10th TN	6th FL
6th KY	15th & 37th TN	7th FL
9th KY	20th TN	1st FL
	30th TN	
	1st TN Bn.	

ARTILLERY: Cobb's KY Battery (Gracey); TN Battery (Mebane); Slocomb's LA Battery

Stevenson's Division

BROWN'S BDE	CUMMING'S BDE	PETTUS'S BDE	VAUGHN'S BDE
3rd TN	34th GA	20th AL	3rd TN
18th & 26th TN	36th GA	23rd AL	39th TN
32nd TN	39th GA	30th AL	43rd TN
45th & 23rd TN	56th GA	31st AL	59th TN
		46th AL	

ARTILLERY: TN Battery (Baxter); TN Battery (Carnes); GA Battery (Van Den Corput); GA Battery (Rowan)

Wheeler's Cavalry Corps

Wharton's Division		**Martin's Division**	
1ST BDE (Harrison)	2ND BDE (Davidson)	1ST BDE (J. T. Morgan)	2ND BDE (Morrison)
3rd AR	1st TN	1st AL	1st GA
65th NC	2nd TN	3rd AL	2nd GA
8th TX	4th TN	4th AL	3rd GA
11th TX	6th TN	Malone's AL Regt.	4th GA
	11th TN	51st AL	6th GA

Armstrong's Division		Kelly's Division	
1ST BDE (Humes)	2ND BDE (Tyler)	1ST BDE (Wade)	2ND BDE (Grigsby)
4th TN	Clay's KY Bn.	1st C.S.	2nd KY
5th TN	Edmundson's VA Bn.	3rd C.S.	3rd KY
8th TN	Jessee's KY Bn.	8th C.S.	9th KY
9th TN	Johnson's KY Bn.	10th C.S.	Allison's TN Squadron
10th TN			Hamilton's TN Bn.
			Rucker's Legion

ARTILLERY: TN Battery (Huggins); TN Battery (Huwald); TN Battery (White); AR Battery (Wiggins)

RESERVE ARTILLERY (Robertson): MO Battery (Barret); Havis's GA Battery (Duncan); Lumsden's AL Battery (Cribbs); GA Battery (Massenburg)

You will get much more from your battlefield tour if you take a few minutes to become familiar with the following information and then refer to it as necessary.

The Organization of Civil War Armies

Following is a diagram of the typical organization and range of strength of a Civil War army:

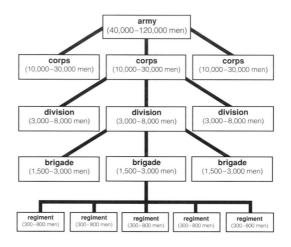

The Basic Battlefield Functions of Civil War Leaders

In combat environments, the duties of Civil War leaders were divided into two main parts: decision making and moral suasion. Although the scope of the decisions varied according to rank and responsibilities, they generally dealt with the movement and deployment of troops, artillery, and logistical support (signal detachments, wagon trains, and so on). Most of the decisions were made by the leaders themselves. Their staffs helped with administrative paperwork but in combat functioned essentially as glorified clerks; they did almost no sifting of intelligence or planning of operations. Once made, the decisions were transmitted to subordinates either by direct exchange or by courier, with the courier either carrying a written order or conveying the order verbally. More rarely, signal flags were used to send instructions. Except in siege operations, when the battle lines were fairly static, the telegraph was almost never used in tactical situations.

Moral suasion was the art of persuading troops to perform their duties and dissuading them from a failure to perform them. This was often done by personal example, and conspicuous bravery was a vital attribute of any good leader. It is therefore not surprising that 8 percent of Union generals—

and 18 percent of their Confederate counterparts–were killed or mortally wounded in action. (By contrast, only about 3 percent of Union enlisted men were killed or mortally wounded in action.)

Although any commander might be called upon to intervene directly on the firing line, army, corps, and division commanders tended to lead from behind the battle line, and their duties were mainly supervisory. In all three cases, their main ability to influence the fighting, once it was under way, was by the husbanding and judicious commitment of troops held in reserve.

Army commanders principally decided the broad questions – whether to attack or defend, where the army's main effort(s) would be made, and when to retreat (or pursue). They made most of their key choices before and after an engagement rather than during it. Once battle was actually joined, their ability to influence the outcome diminished considerably. They might choose to wait it out or they might choose, temporarily and informally, to exercise the function of a lesser leader. In various Civil War battles army commanders conducted themselves in a variety of ways: as detached observers, "super" corps commanders, division commanders, and so on, all the way down to de facto colonels trying to lead through personal example.

Corps commanders chiefly directed main attacks or supervised the defense of large, usually well-defined sectors. It was their function to carry out the broad (or occasionally specific) wishes of the army commander. They coordinated all the elements of their corps (typically infantry divisions and artillery battalions) to maximize its offensive or defensive strength. Once battle was actually joined they influenced the outcome by feeding additional troops into the fight – sometimes by preserving a reserve force (usually a division) and committing it at the appropriate moment, sometimes by requesting additional support from adjacent corps or from the army commander.

Division commanders essentially had the same functions as corps commanders, but on a smaller scale. When attacking, however, their emphasis was less on feeding a fight than keeping the striking power of their divisions as compact as possible. The idea was to strike one hard blow rather than a series of lesser ones.

The commanders below were expected to control the actual combat – to close with and destroy the enemy:

Brigade commanders principally conducted the actual business of attacking or defending. They accompanied the attacking force in person or stayed on the firing line with the defense. Typically they placed about three of their regiments abreast of one another with about two in immediate support. Their job was basically to maximize the fighting power of their brigades by ensuring that these regiments had an unobstructed field of fire and did not overlap. During an attack it often became necessary to expand, contract, or otherwise modify the brigade frontage to conform with the vagaries of terrain, the movements of adjacent friendly brigades, or the behavior of enemy forces. It was the brigade commander's responsibility to shift his regiments as needed while preserving, if possible, the unified striking power of the brigade.

Regiment commanders were chiefly responsible for making their men do as the brigade commanders wished, and their independent authority on the battlefield was limited. For example, if defending they might order a limited counterattack, but they usually could not order a retreat without approval from higher authority. Assisted by *company commanders*, they directly supervised the soldiers, giving specific, highly concrete commands: move this way or that, hold your ground, fire by volley, forward, and so on. Commanders at this level were expected to lead by personal example and to display as well as demand strict adherence to duty.

Civil War Tactics

Civil War armies basically had three kinds of combat troops: infantry, cavalry, and artillery. Infantrymen fought on foot, each with his own weapon. Cavalrymen were trained to fight on horseback or dismounted, also with their own individual weapons. Artillerymen fought with cannon.

INFANTRY

Infantry were by far the most numerous part of a Civil War army and were chiefly responsible for seizing and holding ground.

The basic Civil War tactic was to put a lot of men next to one another in a line and have them move and shoot together. By present-day standards the notion of placing troops shoulder-to-shoulder seems insane, but it still made good sense in the mid-nineteenth century. There were two reasons for this strategy: first, it allowed soldiers to concentrate the fire of their rather limited weapons; second, it was almost the only way to move troops effectively under fire.

Most Civil War infantrymen used muzzle-loading muskets capable of being loaded and fired a maximum of about three times a minute. Individually, therefore, a soldier was nothing. He could affect the battlefield only by combining his fire with that of other infantrymen. Although spreading out made them less vulnerable, infantrymen very quickly lost the ability to combine their fire effectively if they did so. Even more critically, their officers rapidly lost the ability to control them.

For most purposes, the smallest tactical unit on a Civil War battlefield was the regiment. Theoretically composed of about 1,000 officers and men, in reality the average Civil War regiment went into battle with about 300 to 600 men. Whatever its size, however, all members of the regiment had to be able to understand and carry out the orders of their colonel and subordinate officers, who generally could communicate only through voice command. Since in the din and confusion of battle only a few soldiers could actually hear any given command, most got the message chiefly by conforming to the movements of the men immediately around them. Maintaining "touch of elbows"–the prescribed close interval–was indispensable for this crude but vital system to work. In addition, infantrymen were trained to "follow the flag"–the unit and national colors were always conspicuously placed in the front and center of each regiment. Thus, when in doubt as to what maneuver the regiment was trying to carry out, soldiers could look to see the direction the colors were moving. That is one major reason why the post of color-bearer was habitually given to the bravest men in the unit. It was not just an honor; it was insurance that the colors would always move in the direction desired by the colonel.

En route to a battle area, regiments typically moved in a column formation, four men abreast. There was a simple maneuver whereby regiments could very rapidly change from column to line once in the battle area, that is, from a formation designed for ease of movement to one designed to maximize firepower. Regiments normally moved and fought in line of battle–a close-order formation actually composed of two lines, front and rear. Attacking units rarely "charged" in the sense of running full tilt toward the enemy; such a maneuver would promptly destroy the formation as faster men outstripped slower ones and everyone spread out. Instead, a regiment using orthodox tactics would typically step off on an attack moving at a "quick time" rate of 110 steps per minute (at which rate it would cover about 85 yards per minute). Once the force came under serious fire, the rate of advance might be increased to a so-called double-quick time of 165 steps per minute (about 150 yards per minute). Only when the regiment was within a few dozen yards of the defending line would it be ordered to advance at a "run" (a very rapid pace but still not a sprint). Thus a regiment might easily take about ten minutes to "charge" 1,000 yards, even if it did not pause for realignment or execute any further maneuvers en route.

In theory an attacking unit would not stop until it reached the enemy line, if then. The idea was to force back the defenders through the size, momentum, and shock effect of the attacking column. (Fixed bayonets were considered indispensable for maximizing the desired shock effect.) In reality, however, the firepower of the defense eventually led most Civil War regiments to stop and return the fire–often at ranges of less than 100 yards. And very often the "charge" would turn into a stand-up firefight at murderously short range, until one side or the other gave way.

It is important to bear in mind that the above description represents a simplified idea of Civil War infantry combat. As you will see as you visit specific stops, the reality could vary significantly.

ARTILLERY

Second in importance to infantry on most Civil War battlefields was the artillery. Not yet the "killing arm" it would become during World War I, when 70 percent of all casualties were inflicted by shellfire, artillery nevertheless played an important role, particularly on the defense. Cannon fire could break up an infantry attack or dissuade enemy infantry from attacking in the first place. Its mere presence could also reassure friendly infantry and so exert a moral effect that might be as important as its physical effect on the enemy.

The basic artillery unit was the *battery*, a group of between four and six fieldpieces commanded by a captain. Early in the war, batteries tended to be attached to infantry brigades. But over time it was found that they worked best when massed together, and both the Union and Confederate armies presently reorganized their artillery to facilitate this. Eventually both sides maintained extensive concentrations of artillery at corps level or higher. Coordinating the fire of 20 or 30 guns on a single target was not unusual, and occasionally (as in the bombardment that preceded Pickett's Charge at Gettysburg) concentrations of well over 100 guns might be achieved.

Practically all Civil War fieldpieces were muzzle-loaded and superficially appeared little changed from their counterparts in the seventeenth and eighteenth centuries. In fact, however, Civil War artillery was quite modern in two respects. First, advances in metallurgy had resulted in cannon barrels that were much lighter than their predecessors but strong enough to contain more powerful charges. Thus, whereas the typical fieldpiece of the Napoleonic era fired a

6-pound round, the typical Civil War era fieldpiece fired a round double that size, with no loss in ease of handling. Second, recent improvements had resulted in the development of practical rifled fieldpieces that had significantly greater range and accuracy than their smoothbore counterparts.

Civil War fieldpieces could fire a variety of shell types, each with its own preferred usage. *Solid shot* was considered best for battering down structures and for use against massed troops (a single round could sometimes knock down several men like tenpins). *Shell*—rounds that contained an explosive charge and burst into fragments when touched off by a time fuse—were used to set buildings afire or to attack troops behind earthworks or under cover. *Spherical case* was similar to shell except that each round contained musket balls (78 in the case of a 12-pound shot, 38 for a 6-pound shot); it was used against bodies of troops moving in the open at ranges of from 500 to 1,500 yards. At ranges of below 500 yards, the round of choice was *canister*, essentially a metal can containing about 27 cast-iron balls, each 1.5 inches in diameter. As soon as a canister round was fired, the sides of the can would rip away and the cast-iron balls would fly directly into the attacking infantry. In desperate situations double and sometimes even triple charges of canister were used.

As recently as the Mexican War, artillery had been used effectively on the offensive, with fieldpieces rolling forward to advanced positions from which they could blast a hole in the enemy line. The advent of the rifled musket, however, made this tactic dangerous—defending infantry could now pick off artillerists who dared to come so close—and so the artillery had to remain farther back. In theory the greater range and accuracy of rifled cannon might have offset this a bit, but rifled cannon fired comparatively small shells of limited effectiveness against infantry at a distance. The preferred use of artillery on the offensive was therefore not against infantry but against other artillery—what was termed "counterbattery work." The idea was to mass one's own cannon against a few of the enemy's cannon and systematically fire so as to kill the enemy's artillerists and dismount his fieldpieces.

CAVALRY

"Whoever saw a dead cavalryman?" was a byword among Civil War soldiers, a pointed allusion to the fact that the battlefield role played by the mounted arm was often negligible. For example, at the battle of Antietam—the single bloodiest day of the entire war—the Union cavalry suffered exactly 5 men killed and 23 wounded. This was in sharp contrast to the role played by cavalry during the Napoleonic era, when a well-timed cavalry charge could exploit an infantry breakthrough, overrun the enemy's retreating foot soldiers, and convert a temporary advantage into a battlefield triumph.

Why was cavalry not used to better tactical advantage? The best single explanation might be that for much of the war there was simply not enough of it to achieve significant results. Whereas cavalry had made up 20 to 25 percent of Napoleonic armies, in Civil War armies it generally averaged 8 to 10 percent or even less. The paucity of cavalry may be explained, in turn, by its much greater expense compared with infantry. A single horse might easily cost ten times the monthly pay of a Civil War private and necessitated the purchase of saddles, bridles, stirrups, and other gear as well as specialized clothing and equipment for the rider. Moreover, horses required about 26 pounds of feed and forage per day, many times the requirement of an infantryman. In addition, remounts were needed to replace worn-out horses, it took far more training to make an effective cavalryman than an effective infantryman, and there was a widespread belief that the heavily wooded terrain of America would limit opportunities to use cavalry on the battlefield. All in all, it is perhaps no wonder that Civil War armies were late in creating really powerful mounted arms.

Instead, cavalry tended to be used mainly for scouting and raiding, duties that took place away from the battlefields. During major engagements their mission was principally to screen the flanks or to control the rear areas. By 1863, however, the North was beginning to create cavalry forces sufficiently numerous and well armed to play a significant role on the battlefield. At Gettysburg, for example, Union cavalrymen armed with rapid-fire, breech-loading carbines were able to hold a Confederate infantry division at bay for several hours. At Cedar Creek in 1864 a massed cavalry charge late in the day completed the ruin of the Confederate army, and during the Appomattox campaign in 1865 Federal cavalry played a decisive role in bringing Lee's retreating army to bay and forcing its surrender.

Appreciation of the Terrain

The whole point of a battlefield tour is to see the ground over which men actually fought. Understanding the terrain is basic to understanding almost every aspect of a battle. Terrain helps to explain why commanders deployed their troops where they did, why attacks occurred in certain areas and not in others, why some attacks succeeded and others did not.

When defending, Civil War leaders often looked for positions with as many of the following characteristics as possible:

First, it obviously had to be ground from which they could keep the enemy from whatever it was they were ordered to defend.

Second, it should be elevated enough to provide good observation and good fields of fire—they wanted to see as far as possible and sometimes (though not always) to shoot as far as possible. The highest ground was not necessarily the best, however, for it often afforded an attacker defilade—areas of ground which the defenders' weapons could not reach. For that reason leaders seldom placed their troops at the very top of a ridge or hill (the "geographical crest"). Instead they placed them a bit forward of the geographical crest at a point from which they had the best field of fire (the "military crest"). Alternatively, they might choose to place their troops behind the crest so as to conceal the size and exact deployment of the defenders from the enemy and offer protection from long-range fire. It also meant that an attacker, upon reaching the crest, would be silhouetted against the sky and susceptible to a sudden, potentially destructive fire at close range.

Third, the ground adjacent to the chosen position should present a potential attacker with obstacles. Streams and ravines made good obstacles because they required an attacker to halt temporarily while trying to cross them. Fences and boulder fields could also slow an attacker. Dense woodlands could do the same, but they offered concealment for potential attackers and were therefore less desirable. In addition to its other virtues, elevated ground was also prized because attackers moving uphill had to exert themselves more and got tired faster. Obstacles were especially critical at the end of a unit's position—the flank—if there were no other units beyond to protect it. That is why commanders "anchored" their flanks, whenever possible, on hills or the banks of large streams.

Fourth, it had to offer ease of access for reinforcements to arrive and, if necessary, for the defenders to retreat.

Fifth, a source of drinkable water—the more the better—should be immediately behind the position if possible. This was especially important for cavalry and artillery units, which had horses to think about as well as men.

When attacking, Civil War commanders looked for different things:

First, they looked for weaknesses in the enemy's position, especially "unanchored" flanks. If there were no obvious weaknesses, they looked for a key point in the enemy's position—often a piece of elevated ground whose loss would undermine the rest of the enemy's defensive line.

Second, they searched for ways to get close to the enemy position without being observed. Using woodlands and ridge lines to screen their movements was a common tactic.

Third, they looked for open, elevated ground on which they could deploy artillery to "soften up" the point to be attacked.

Fourth, once the attack was under way they tried, when possible, to find areas of defilade in which their troops could gain relief from exposure to enemy fire. Obviously it was almost never possible to find defilade that offered protection all the way to the enemy line, but leaders could often find some point en route where they could pause briefly to "dress" their lines.

Making the best use of terrain was an art that almost always involved trade-offs among these various factors—and also required consideration of the number of troops available. Even a very strong position was vulnerable if there were not enough troops to defend it. A common error among Civil War generals, for example, was to stretch their line too thin in order to hold an otherwise desirable piece of ground.

Estimating Distance

When touring Civil War battlefields it's often helpful to have a general sense of distance. For example, estimating distance can help you estimate how long it took troops to get from point A to point B or to visualize the points at which they would have become vulnerable to different kinds of artillery fire. There are several easy tricks to bear in mind.

—Use reference points for which the exact distance is known. Many battlefield stops give you the exact distance to one or more key points in the area. Locate such a reference point, then try to divide the intervening terrain into equal parts. For instance, say the reference point is 800 yards away. The ground about halfway in between will be 400 yards; the ground halfway between you and the midway point will be 200 yards, and so on.

—Use the football field method. Visualize the length of a football field, which of course is 100 yards. Then estimate the number of football fields you could put between yourself and the distant point in which you're interested.

—Use cars, houses, and other common objects that tend to be roughly the same size. Most cars are about the same size and so are many houses. Become familiar with how large or small such objects appear at various distances—300 yards, 1,000 yards, 2,000 yards, and so on. This is a less accurate way of estimating distance, but can be helpful if the lay of the land makes it otherwise hard to tell whether a point is near or far. Look for such objects that seem a bit in front of the point. Their relative size can give you a useful clue.

Maximum Effective Ranges of Common Civil War Weapons

Rifled musket	400 yds.
Smoothbore musket	150 yds.
Breech-loading carbine	300 yds.
Napoleon 12-pounder smoothbore cannon	
Solid shot	1,700 yds.
Shell	1,300 yds.
Spherical case	500 – 1,500 yds.
Canister	400 yds.
Parrott 10-pounder rifled cannon	
Solid shot	6,000 yds.
3-inch ordnance rifle (cannon)	
Solid shot	4,000 yds.

Further Reading

Coggins, Jack. *Arms and Equipment of the Civil War*. 1962. Reprint. Wilmington NC: Broadfoot Books, 1990.

The best introduction to the subject, engagingly written, profusely illustrated, and packed with information.

Griffith, Paddy. *Battle Tactics of the Civil War*. New Haven: Yale University Press, 1989.

Griffith argues that in a tactical sense, the Civil War was more nearly the last great Napoleonic war rather than the first modern war. In his view, the impact of the rifled musket on Civil War battlefields has been exaggerated; the carnage and inconclusiveness of many Civil War battles owed less to the inadequacy of Napoleonic tactics than to a failure to understand and apply them.

Jamieson, Perry D. *Crossing the Deadly Ground: United States Army Tactics, 1865 – 1899*. Tuscaloosa: University of Alabama Press, 1994.

The early chapters offer a good analysis of the tactical lessons learned by U.S. army officers from their Civil War experiences.

Linderman, Gerald F. *Embattled Courage: The Experience of Combat in the American Civil War*. New York: Free Press, 1987.

A thoughtful, well-written study of how Civil War soldiers understood and coped with the challenges of the battlefield.

McWhiney, Grady, and Perry D. Jamieson. *Attack and Die: Civil War Military Tactics and the Southern Heritage*. Tuscaloosa: University of Alabama Press, 1982.

Although unconvincing in its assertion that their Celtic heritage led Southerners to take the offensive to an inordinate degree, this is a excellent tactical study that emphasizes the revolutionary impact of the rifled musket. Best read in combination with Griffith, above.

Counting the Scars in the Colors. BLCW 3:284

Sources	In general, the works cited in the "For Further Reading" sections of each stop provide information, interpretation, and insight, and the citing of those works in that section should in every case be taken as an attribution of credit for the material thus used. Sources for specific items follow.

Chickamauga

Stop 2	The quotation in the vignette is from Benjamin Scribner, *How Soldiers Were Made; or, the War as I Saw It Under Buell, Rosecrans, Thomas, Grant and Sherman* (Chicago: Donohue and Henneberry, 1887), 148.
Stop 3	The exchange between Corp. William Atkins and Capt. G. W. Lewis is from George W. Lewis, *The Campaigns of the One Hundred Twenty-fourth Ohio Volunteer Infantry* (Akron: Werner, 1894), 57.
Stop 4	Wilder's statement about the execution his guns were doing to the Confederates in front of his position is from his report in *War of the Rebellion: Official Records of the Union and Confederate Armies*, 128 vols. (Washington DC: Government Printing Office, 1881–1901), vol. 30, pt. 1, p. 447 (hereinafter OR; all citations are from series I).
Stop 5	The story of Bate's promotion is from Tucker, *Chickamauga*, 181.
Stop 6	Ambrose Bierce's description of the fighting in Poe Field is from *The Collected Works of Ambrose Bierce*, 10 vols. (New York: Gordian Press, 1966), 1:271–72.
Stop 7	The quotation from D. H. Hill is from his report, OR, 30, pt. 2, p. 140.
Stop 8	The John Beatty quotation is from his *Memoirs of a Volunteer, 1861–1863*, ed. Harvey S. Ford (New York: Norton, 1946), 246.
Stop 10	The soldier who described General Helm's demeanor before the battle was John S. Jackman in *Diary of a Confederate Soldier: John S. Jackman of the Orphan Brigade*, ed. William C. Davis (Columbia: University of South Carolina Press, 1990), 88.
Stop 12	General Hazen's statement is from his report, OR, 30, pt. 1, pp. 763–64.

Stop 14	Bushrod Johnson's statement is from his report, *OR*, 30, pt. 2, pp. 457–58.
Stop 15	Colonel Lyman Bennett's description of the scene he viewed from the top of Lytle Hill is from Lyman G. Bennett, *History of the Thirty-sixth Regiment Illinois Volunteers During the War of the Great Rebellion* (Aurora IL: Knickerbocker and Hodder, 1876).
Stop 16	Colonel Atkins's assessment of Assistant Secretary of War Dana is quoted in Cozzens, *This Terrible Sound*, 396.
Stop 18	The quotation by Peter Cozzens is from *This Terrible Sound*, 422. The Opdyke-Thomas exchange is from Charles Clark, *Opdycke Tigers, 125th O.V.I., a History of the Regiment and the Campaigns and Battles of the Army of the Cumberland* (Columbus: Spahr and Glenn, 1895), 117.
Stop 19	The quotations in the vignette are from Beatty, *Memoirs of a Volunteer*, 250–51.
Stop 20	The Tennessee soldier's recollection is quoted in Cozzens, *This Terrible Sound*, 501; Bierce's is from *Collected Works*, 1:277–78.
Optional Excursion 1	Minty's exchange with Mrs. Reed is to be found in Joseph Vale, *Minty and the Cavalry: A History of Cavalry Campaigns in the Western Armies* (Harrisburg PA: Edwin K. Meyers, 1886), 226–27.
Optional Excursion 2	Cummings's friendly postwar chafing of Wilder is quoted in Cozzens, *This Terrible Sound*, 113.
Optional Excursion 5	The Confederate soldier who was appalled at the carnage where Cleburne had fought was John S. Jackman, and his description is to be found in *Diary of a Confederate Soldier*, 88.
Optional Excursion 6	The quotation from John B. Hood is from the report of Bushrod Johnson, *OR*, 30, pt. 2, p. 458. The quotation from Charles Harker is from his report, *OR*, 30, pt. 1, p. 695. The statement of Lt. Charles Clark is quoted in Cozzens, *This Terrible Sound*, 413.
Optional Excursion 7	Lt. Wilson Vance's description of the fighting on Horseshoe Ridge is from his report, *OR*, 30, pt. 1, p. 496.

Chattanooga

Introduction	The quotation at the end of the introduction is from Beatty, *Memoirs of a Volunteer*, 272.

Stop 1   The first Federal officer's quote in stop 1a is from Chesley A. Mosman, *The Rough Side of War: The Civil War Journal of Chesley A. Mosman, 1st Lieutenant, Company D, 59th Illinois Volunteer Infantry Regiment*, ed. Arnold Gates (Garden City NY: Basin Publishing, 1987), 90–91. The second is from Beatty, *Memoirs of a Volunteer*, 258.

Stop 2   The poem "Charge of the Mule Brigade" is quoted in McDonough, *Chattanooga*, 92–93.

Stop 3   Of the three quotations in the vignette, the first two appear in Cozzens, *Shipwreck of Their Hopes*, 200, and the third is from the report of Brig. Gen. Charles Cruft, *OR*, 31, pt. 2, p. 309.

Stop 6   The statement by the Confederate soldier is quoted in Sword, *Mountains Touched with Fire*, 246.

Stop 7   Van Derveer's description of the storming of the ridge is from his report, *OR*, 31, pt. 1, p. 528. Axel Reed's statement is quoted in Cozzens, *Shipwreck of Their Hopes*, 329.

Optional Excursion 1   Manigault's statement is from *A Carolinian Goes to War: The Civil War Narrative of Arthur Middleton Manigault, Brigadier General, C.S.A.*, ed. R. Lockwood Tower (Columbia: University of South Carolina Press, 1988), 137.

Confederate Roll-Call.
BLCW 4:205

Suggestions for Further Reading

The Chickamauga and Chattanooga campaigns are the subject of a number of recent studies. I have written a brief account of the battle of Chickamauga entitled *A Deep Steady Thunder: The Battle of Chickamauga* (Fort Worth: Ryan Place, 1996) and another on the battle of Chattanooga, *This Grand Spectacle: The Battle of Chattanooga* (Abilene TX: McWhiney Foundation Press, 1999), as well as a much larger and more analytical study of the entire struggle for Tennessee in late 1863, from Tullahoma to Knoxville, entitled *Six Armies in Tennessee: The Chickamauga and Chattanooga Campaigns* (Lincoln: University of Nebraska Press, 1998).

Glen Tucker's *Chickamauga: Bloody Battle in the West* (Indianapolis: Bobbs-Merrill, 1961) is by now outdated and contains some inaccuracies but is still useful and entertaining to read. Peter Cozzens's *This Terrible Sound: The Battle of Chickamauga* (Urbana: University of Illinois Press, 1992) is highly detailed and interesting.

Chattanooga has received even more attention in the last few years than has Chickamauga. The best of the recent major studies of the battle is Wiley Sword's *Mountains Touched with Fire: Chattanooga Besieged, 1863* (New York: St. Martin's, 1995). Another good account is Cozzens's *The Shipwreck of Their Hopes: The Battles for Chattanooga* (Urbana: University of Illinois Press, 1994). A slightly older and somewhat briefer account that is still valuable, insightful, and enjoyable reading is James Lee McDonough's *Chattanooga—A Death Grip on the Confederacy* (Knoxville: University of Tennessee Press, 1984). The rapid transfer of Union troops that brought Hooker's force to the Chattanooga area in time for the battle is the subject of Roger Pickenpaugh's *Rescue by Rail* (Lincoln: University of Nebraska Press, forthcoming). Edward Carr Franks provides a highly analytical reexamination of Bragg's detachment of Longstreet to East Tennessee in "The Detachment of Longstreet Considered: Braxton Bragg, James Longstreet, and the Chattanooga Campaign," in *Leadership and Command in the American Civil War*, ed. Steven E. Woodworth (Campbell CA: Savas, 1996).

Several of the figures in this campaign are the subjects of excellent biographies. Bruce Catton's *Grant Takes Command* (Boston: Little, Brown, 1968) is the best treatment of that general's military operations during this period. John Marszalek deals ably with Grant's most trusted lieutenant in *Sherman: A Soldier's Passion for Order* (New York: Free Press, 1993). The available works on Rosecrans and Thomas are badly outdated and in need of replacement, but for now the best biographies are William Lamers's *The Edge of Glory: A Biography of General William S. Rosecrans, U.S.A.* (New York: Harcourt, Brace, and World, 1961) and Francis McKinney's *Education in Violence: The Life of George H. Thomas and the History of the Army of the Cumberland* (Detroit: Wayne State University Press, 1961).

Prominent Confederates have also had their biographers. Judith Lee Hallock focuses on Bragg's difficult relations with his subordinates in *Braxton Bragg and Confederate Defeat*, vol. 2 (Tuscaloosa: University of Alabama Press, 1991). Nathaniel Cheairs Hughes has written a fine and well-balanced biography of one of those subordinates in *General William J. Hardee: Old Reliable* (Baton Rouge: Louisiana State University Press, 1965). A long-awaited modern, high-quality biography of Cleburne is now available thanks to Craig Symonds, who has written *Stonewall of the West* (Lawrence: University Press of Kansas, 1997). The careers of some of Bragg's other subordinates are chronicled in Joseph H. Parks, *General Leonidas Polk, C.S.A.: The Fighting Bishop* (Baton Rouge: Louisiana State University Press, 1962), William C. Davis's *John C. Breckinridge: Statesman, Soldier, Symbol* (Baton Rouge: Louisiana State University Press, 1974), and Jeffry D. Wert, *General James Longstreet: The Confederacy's Most Controversial Soldier—A Biography* (New York: Simon & Schuster, 1993). The last of these, while very well researched and written, is quite sympathetic to Longstreet, so a suitable antidote might be Judith Lee Hallock's *General James Longstreet in the West: A Monumental Failure* (Fort Worth: Ryan Place, 1996). Hal Bridges, *Lee's Maverick General: Daniel Harvey Hill* (1961; reprint, Lincoln: University of Nebraska Press, 1991) is a highly sympathetic account of a general who proved difficult for Bragg as well.

Confederate strategy and the difficult personal relationships that complicated Southern efforts in this campaign are part of the subject of my own *Jefferson Davis and His Generals: The Failure of Confederate Command in the West* (Lawrence: University Press of Kansas, 1990). Another work that deals extensively with the Confederate decision to concentrate forces against Rosecrans in the late summer of 1863 is Thomas L. Connelly and Archer Jones's *The Politics of Command: Factions and Ideas in Confederate Strategy* (Baton Rouge: Louisiana State University Press, 1982). Connelly's *Autumn of Glory: The Army of Tennessee, 1862–1865* (Baton Rouge: Louisiana State University Press, 1971) offers a critical account of the high command of the Confederacy's chief western army during the years mentioned in the title.

Finally, for a different sort of tour of the Chickamauga battlefield, you may want to try Matt Spruill's *Guide to the*

Battle of Chickamauga (Lawrence: University Press of Kansas, 1993). Aside from directions to the stops and very brief explanatory notes, Spruill's guide is composed entirely of excerpts from the writing of participants, mostly their reports of the battle.

Confederate sharpshooter. BLCW 2:202

In the This Hallowed Ground: Guides to Civil War Battlefields series

Chickamauga: A Battlefield Guide
with a section on Chattanooga
Steven E. Woodworth

Gettysburg: A Battlefield Guide
Mark Grimsley and Brooks D. Simpson